ADVANCE PRAISE

"*Sujin* Lee's journey breaks the mould of the conventional tech entrepreneur narrative, focusing not just on his achievements but on the resilience and purpose that fuelled his path. Unlike many of his peers, Lee came from an atypical startup background, yet he navigated through these challenges with remarkable acumen. His refusal to accept the status quo and his dedication to pushing beyond traditional measures of success led him to embrace a progressive approach to business growth. This mindset spurred his company into a period of rapid expansion, setting it apart from competitors and establishing a unique value proposition. Lee's willingness to invest in the early struggles laid a robust foundation for a business that scaled more swiftly and solidly than many others in the field. His continuous quest for excellence and relentless questioning of what constitutes 'enough' signals that the current achievements are merely the groundwork for future endeavours. Lee's high standards and perpetual drive for improvement are key to his company's ongoing development and success."

Saeju Jeong
Founder, Noom

Published by
LID Publishing
An imprint of LID Business Media Ltd.
LABS House, 15-19 Bloomsbury Way,
London, WC1A 2TH, UK

info@lidpublishing.com
www.lidpublishing.com

A member of:

BPR ✿
businesspublishersroundtable.com

Printed and bound in Great Britain by Halstan Ltd
ISBN: 978-1-915951-49-6
ISBN: 978-1-915951-50-2 (ebook)

Cover and page design: Caroline Li

AN ENTREPRENEUR'S JOURNEY
FROM MOTEL JANITOR TO
CEO OF A GLOBAL ENTERPRISE

RESTART

SUJIN LEE

LID

MADRID | MEXICO CITY | LONDON
BUENOS AIRES | BOGOTA | SHANGHAI

ABOUT THE AUTHOR

This is not a memoir written retrospectively after success. It is Sujin Lee's management journal, candidly documenting his journey through the first 19 years of running his business, Yanolja. This management diary chronicles the founder's intense endeavour to grow the company into a decacorn. Starting in his 20s, he jotted down his future goals and, as you turn the pages of this book, it will soon become evident how these goals were transformed into reality. Organized chronologically, this journal provides an insight into the growth and success of the company. Spanning 2005–2023, it captures the founder's initial concerns, challenges faced at various milestones, establishment and resilience during crises, and his unwavering determination and passion, all of which were highlighted during the company's 10th anniversary in 2015. This 19-year narrative not only reveals the fulfilment of his visions, but also his achievements beyond them.

The book captures how he started out with nothing, cleaning motels, before founding a business with only two desks and $50,000 in capital, growing it by more than 150% annually, until its valuation reached tens of millions of dollars. By 2015, the company's valuation hit $200 million after receiving its first $200 million investment. This growth accelerated with a $2 billion investment from Soft Bank Vision Fund 2, catapulting the corporate value to $10 billion and establishing it as a decacorn. It also details his partnership with Lee Beom-seok, the general director, who invested $10 million when the company was valued at $200 million, along with CEOs Kim Jong-yoon and Bae Bo-chan. Kim Jong-yoon, the pathfinder, and Bae Bo-chan, the trailblazing genius, played pivotal roles in the company's development. Additionally, the author reveals the formation of the current organizational structure, including his position of CEO, where he is described as a fearless fighter, and his contributions to Yanolja's dynamic leadership team.

Being a compilation of journal entries, *Restart* offers the author's candid, honest confessions, without flashy rhetoric. It's a rare find, vividly but truthfully depicting a company's growth. As a raw, unprocessed record, it is without dramatic development, but its authenticity makes it an invaluable reference for those preparing to start or are already running a company. It also serves as a source of motivation for those who might have lost their passion or feel adrift.

Remember, if you don't give up – and take up the challenge after each failure – your vision will become a reality.

Starting from zero, every step forward and every drop of sweat can pave the way to success.

Sujin Lee defines himself as a "man who always tries." He had a difficult childhood, raised by his grandmother after his father died when he was four and his mother remarried and left him when he was six. It was hard for him to learn to read and write Korean because he was busy helping his grandmother with farming. He was only able to do so when he reached the fifth grade, having received intensive help from his teacher.

His academic performance was always low. But while in junior high, he delivered newspapers, during which time he was fortunate to receive free tutoring from a college student, enabling him to improve his school grades.

He then studied mechanical drafting at Anseong Doowon Technical High School and went on to study and graduate from the mould department of Cheonan Technical College (currently Cheonan College of Engineering at Kongju University). After graduating, he was exempt from military service because he worked as an industrial technician at a defense company. Before he was 20, he moved to Seoul with nothing but his bare hands as assets. He worked as a motel cleaner until, in 2005, at the age of 28, he co-founded a business with a younger friend, with a capital of $50,000. He is now a leader in the global travel industry, spearheading the lodging sector and creating a culture, but there have been many difficulties during his 19 years in business.

There was a time when all his employees, except for the vice president, quit en masse and joined a competitor. He then lost the trademark rights to Motel Tour (MoTu) – which had barely broken even – to the same competitor. Due to his lack of knowledge, he lost the trademark rights when the company was just beginning to profit and show potential for growth. These crises meant he had to start again from scratch, a situation akin to a death sentence for his business. Eventually, he relinquished the MoTu trademark and created a new one, Yanolja, in August 2006. This moment marked a crisis morphing into an opportunity. Since then, he has been growing his business, forging ahead unshaken and undeterred, no matter what crises he's faced.

In 2024, 19 years after founding his company, Yanolja is a global travel tech company. The company is transitioning from an online to mobile business, and further into a cloud-based tech business in the Online-to-offline (O2O) service market, providing lodging and travel services. Starting from the bottom with nothing, he kept moving forward step-by-step, with every drop of sweat enriching his life. His efforts and challenges continue to this day.

Since his 20s, he has doggedly persevered, constantly reminding himself that "all I have to do is refuse to ever give up." Every time he faced failure, he rose up and started again, turning each setback into a steppingstone. Whenever he succeeded, he didn't rest on his laurels but moved forward, aiming for greater achievements. Throughout his life, he has been living proof that anyone can shape their destiny as long as they don't give up, regardless of the situation.

He was a man whose chances of success were deemed very low by worldly standards. Yet, he defied those odds. Throughout *Restart*, you will find yourself thinking, "If he could do it, so can I."

CONTENTS

Note

All amounts are converted based on the rate of

1 dollar = 1,000 won.

PREFACE
TO THE REVISED EDITION
ENVISIONING A GLOBAL TOP-TIER TRAVEL TECH COMPANY

I have received several copies of *Restart* from my readers, which I keep in a corner of my office. These copies are filled with underlining and notes, showing the engagement of the readers. It's remarkable that this book, first published in 2015, continues to sell in 2024. I often receive emails with book reviews, and sometimes, these books are sent to me as gifts. I am deeply grateful for this, as it indicates that my readers have found my book inspirational during challenging times, when embarking on new beginnings, or when aspiring to achieve wealth and success.

Restart is a compilation of my thoughts and experiences in business management, as the founder of Yanolja, 2005–2014. I updated and modified parts of my business journals for the March 2015 publication of *Restart*, which marked a recommitment to my initial resolve – to persevere with unwavering determination.

The business journals consist of posts I shared over the course of ten years with Yanolja employees via our internal bulletin board. The content varies in appeal depending on the reader's perspective, and none of it is sugar-coated. That's why some people say this is a unique book. My intention was not to publish these writings publicly; they were meant to communicate my message across the organization, to help employees understand our business, and continually motivate and inspire myself. Many entries include specific dates and times, indicating that they were written spontaneously to capture my genuine feelings, rather than as reflections after Yanolja's success.

These journal entries were written by me as I constantly sought growth, envisioning the future while progressively building the company. Everything I aimed to achieve, almost as if casting spells on myself while sharing with my employees, soon became a reality. My experience of visions turning into reality continue to this day. I am still envisioning. People often ask me, "What's your plan now?" Some say I should be satisfied with my achievements. But most people are curious about what I plan to do next.

There are three reasons for publishing a revised edition of *Restart*. The first is that I wanted to conduct an interim review. Curiosity about our vision, dreams, and future indicates interest in and belief in our future. I feel a profound sense of responsibility and pride in leading an organization that turns visions into reality, an organization that continuously envisions a greater, more definitive future. We still have much to accomplish; I started with nothing, and I aimed to earn $300 million. During my pursuit of this goal, there were times when $300 million seemed like a modest sum. Eventually, my employees and I surpassed that goal by a significant margin. Despite the world grappling with rising inflation and interest rates, my approach remains unchanged. It is challenging to stand out among numerous global companies, but we persistently embrace these challenges. By continuously setting higher goals, we aim to eventually occupy a central position in the global travel industry. Achieving this makes a $300 billion target seem attainable, a notion some might find absurd.

When I resolved to earn $300 million in my 20s without any financial backing, even close friends dismissed it as unrealistic and not worth considering. Their skepticism was understandable given the improbability at the time, but I was always forward-looking. Even after securing our first investment and setting a sales target exceeding one billion, skepticism persisted. Critics questioned how a company with $20 million in sales could aim for one billion, suggesting that a corporate value of one billion would be more realistic. But that was the investment company's view. We strived to grow sustainably and be self-sustaining. As we progress, a billion in sales is no longer our goal. I understand that perspectives vary, whether from friends or investment companies, but ultimately, it's not about them; it's about how I see myself and how we shape our own destiny.

Some might question, "Why aim for $300 billion?" This figure represents the threshold for market leadership in the global travel industry. Currently, the benchmark is $100 billion, but as the industry grows, I believe $300 billion will be the future standard for industry leadership. This leading position will eventually become reality, and if its existence is inevitable, striving for it seems justified. I am reaffirming my commitment to this journey, viewing it as an opportunity for continuous self-improvement and collective growth.

The second reason for publishing a new edition of *Restart* is to reorganize the 2015 version in a more systematic way. On a flight to Singapore, I read an annotated copy of *Restart* sent by a reader. I decided that restructuring the timeline would make the book more accessible and useful to those facing challenges. I also wanted to convey to my readers that, even eight years after its initial publication, my process of self-challenge and progress remains unchanged, as it yields continuous improvement and growth.

The third reason is to support young entrepreneurs facing tough times. Everyone is struggling in the current climate, working hard but often not receiving adequate feedback. Having faced numerous challenges myself, I know that it's challenging to provide advice tailored to each unique situation, even with my extensive business experience and management background. I thought that my past writings, organized chronologically, might offer some guidance, and alleviate their thirst for advice.

This book is significant not just because it reflects the magnitude of wealth or success, but because it encapsulates my entire life philosophy and spirit. I hope that this revised edition of *Restart* serves as a modest milestone for those who are searching for their path.

SUJIN LEE
MARCH 2023

PREFACE
TO THE FIRST EDITION
ANYONE CAN CHANGE THEIR DESTINY

Over the past ten years of running a business, I have encountered numerous failures and setbacks. I had no formal management training and am not adept at using indicators. My educational background doesn't necessarily equip me to respond wisely to various situations. These are points I often discuss when invited as a speaker.

Reflecting on myself, I see an introverted, quick-witted, and strong individual. I am neither smarter nor more capable than others, and I am aware of this. Considering who I am, can you imagine the hardships and trials I faced during a decade of business management?

This book brings together the conflicts I faced, the thoughts I had at critical moments, and the action guidelines I followed. These insights vividly capture the ups and downs I experienced when starting and managing a business at a young age, with little knowledge.

Disclosing my writings was not an easy task. If it were merely about refining my thoughts into an essay, it would have been straightforward. However, knowing that my family, friends and colleagues will read this book, I couldn't lie or make up situations. Deciding on the extent of disclosure was also challenging. I hope this record serves as evidence of the struggles I faced in life, starting a business from scratch and achieving what I have before turning 40, all while striving to establish my identity.

I hope this evidence will inspire the Yanolja family, their friends, their families and those seeking hope. *Restart* is a collection of writings that I have shared with Yanolja employees. For ten years, I openly posted these words on the company bulletin board whenever I had concerns or ideas about the company.

There were so many, it was impossible to include them all. However, I tried to include entries that marked important points. As a rule, I refrained from editing them, except for correcting typos. This was because I wanted to share sincere writings that would provide guidance to our Yanolja employees, offer clarity to myself, and be of help to young people, those with passion, and those in need of hope.

Now they are being shared with the world, I feel motivated to work even harder. Perhaps not many are concerned with who Sujin Lee, the founder of Yanolja, is, but this book chronicles how I have lived in the past and what I plan to do in the future. In that sense, *Restart* is my commitment to moving forward.

I have briefly mentioned my childhood, youth and experiences working as a motel cleaner before starting my own business. Through these recollections, you'll see that my life has not been easy, and I did not grow up in a privileged environment. Yet, I have managed to come this far. My journey to this point is not because I am superior to others, but because I believe everyone has the potential to change their circumstances.

I was someone considered highly unlikely to succeed. However, I managed to defy those low expectations. Instead of approaching this book with the preconceived notion of Sujin Lee being a self-made man, I hope you read it and adopt a positive mindset. Tell yourself, "If he can do it, so can I."

CHAPTER 1

RESTART ONCE AGAIN

2022
EIGHTEENTH YEAR SINCE FOUNDING

REFLECTING ON A NEW MILESTONE

On March 20, 2022, I boarded a plane to the United States, a trip I had been thinking about for a long time. In truth, I could have embarked on this journey much earlier. I had the financial means and plenty of reasons to go. What I lacked, however, was courage.

My first visit to New York was in 2016. That trip could have been just for pleasure, but I sought a more meaningful experience. I wanted to meet my younger sister, if only briefly, who had been adopted as a child and was living in America. I was also keen to observe firsthand the dynamics of the American market.

During a dinner with some young startup founders, I suggested, "Shall we go and check out America?" While Silicon Valley in San Francisco, with its multitude of IT startups, had much to teach me, I had never been to the rest of the U.S. The allure of the vibrant city of New York was compelling. So, I convinced the startup CEOs to join me and purchased economy class tickets to New York on Asiana Airlines.

As an adult, while working in the defense industry as an alternative to mandatory military service, I reached out to Holt Children's Services, an international adoption agency, in search of my sister and anxiously awaited a response. Around that time, I learned that a group of Korean adoptees, now adults, were visiting Korea to connect with their heritage. There was a chance my sister might be among them. However, the thought of meeting her filled me with apprehension: I didn't speak English, she presumably didn't speak Korean, and I was struggling financially, living in my aunt's house.

And I had no memories of my sister – our long separation and my lack of notable achievements made me feel embarrassed and unprepared for a reunion.

As the day of the potential reunion with my younger sister drew closer, my anxiety intensified to the point where I regretted ever initiating the search. I learned that my sister expressed a desire to visit the Jecheon Infant Home, where she had been cared for before her adoption. So, I travelled from Seoul to the Jecheon Infant Home. At the time, I was employed by a lighting manufacturing and export company, and I asked a close colleague in the trade department to act as my interpreter. Asking for this assistance in my early 20s was a humbling experience; revealing my family history exposed my deepest vulnerabilities.

When I finally met my sister, all the worry, anxiety and fear seemed to vanish, replaced only by tears. Without uttering a single word, we embraced and wept together. I had never cried so intensely in my life. During my freshman year of junior high, I wept ceaselessly at my grandmother's funeral — she had raised me as an orphan. But even those tears were not as profuse as they were upon seeing my sister for the first time.

I returned to Seoul with my sister, introduced her to my relatives, and took some photographs. I spent two days accompanying her as she explored Korea. That was the last time I saw her before our next meeting in New York, six years ago, after a gap of 18 years.

During my stay in New York, I visited and toured the office of the startup Noom. I stayed in an Airbnb located in a predominantly Black neighbourhood and spent much of my time simply exploring the city on foot, sometimes covering as much as 20 miles in a day.

The others in the group, all young startup founders, occasionally showed signs of fatigue, but I was determined to experience New York to the fullest. I toured the New York Stock Exchange, but found myself hesitating to enter, standing in front of the building for a long time. My reasons for visiting New York were manifold: to visit a few successful innovative startups, to reunite with my younger sister, and to immerse myself in the life of a New Yorker. And seeing the New York Stock Exchange, the capital market's mecca, was one of the big reasons.

I started my business with just two desks in an apartment in Uijeongbu. Two years later, I moved the office to a small officetel on Teheran-ro in the heart of Gangnam, Seoul. During that time, as part of a small team of fewer than ten people, I often walked down Teheran Road, amid towering buildings, dreaming of ambitious business ventures. My route stretched from Seolleung, past Yeoksam Station, to Gangnam Station. My major clients, primarily lodging business owners who were also my main advertising partners, were located in areas around Seolleung Station, Yeoksam Station, and Gangnam Station. Walking these streets was not only enjoyable but also gave me the opportunity to closely observe the alleys of the commercial district, allowing me to analyse which stores attracted customers. I could then apply these insights to my own business, thereby enhancing the likelihood of success.

As my employees and I walked down Teheran Road, we timidly promised ourselves that one day our company would grow large enough to occupy an entire floor of those towering buildings. Such grand dreams were possible because we were in the early, naive stages of our business journey. Ten years on from that dream of occupying a full floor on Teheran-ro, we realized our ambition. In fact, our company had grown so significantly, it occupied half of the buildings along Teheran-ro.

Like my experience in 2016, standing in front of the New York Stock Exchange Building, I quietly vowed to one day display my business's symbol on the wall of such an esteemed building. I remember taking a photo with the Charging Bull statue, reinforcing my determination with the thought, "I can do this. I resolve to make it happen someday." Thus, my trip to New York was meaningful in many ways. Six years later, on March 20, 2022, I found myself boarding a plane to the United States once again. Many things had changed. Six years earlier, I was with startup founders, and I recall how everyone in the group grumbled about enduring a 14-hour flight in uncomfortable seats, finding a cramped room through Airbnb, and scrimping on meals.

Even though my sister was adopted in America, I had been too indifferent to learn English. But now, I am the owner of a global company that offers hotel management solutions in more than 60 languages across 180 countries. Of course, I'm still learning English and have yet to master it. Despite receiving substantial investments, I am not leading a life of luxury; I am continually striving for greater growth.

How did I manage to come this far? Before I forget, I want to think about and understand the journey from my past to the present. I also aim to create an

opportunity where I must contemplate and acknowledge my new milestones.

March 22, 2022

2023
NINETEENTH YEAR SINCE FOUNDING

NOW IT'S WINTER,
BUT SOON IT'LL BE SPRING

There's still a long way to go. Many people view us as a big company capable of much more, yet we remain a modest presence. There are numerous tasks at hand, and we're all diligently seeking the right way to accomplish them.

My team and I have been steering Yanolja for 18 years. However, now seems to be the time when our thirst for progress is at its peak. Admittedly, we possess both capital and talent, and the company has been on a growth trajectory annually. You might wonder, "Then, what's the problem?" The issue, as I see it, is our complacency in being the industry leader – a status we've achieved both consciously and unconsciously. This success has made us larger and, consequently, slower. Despite reaching our long-sought goals, it's challenging to recapture the unified sense of vision and dream that was so palpable when we started from scratch. Many leaders raise concerns about what shouldn't be done, yet struggle to find or implement solutions.

I've pondered deeply about the root of this issue. Was it because we lost touch with each other's perspectives during three years of non-contact, online meetings and tasks due to the COVID-19 pandemic? Or is it the illusion of productivity that working from home creates? Or perhaps joining a company leads to complacency and a diminished hunger for growth? At the end of this reflection, I realized the problem lies with me. As the founder, people often mistakenly call me the chairman or president. But I remain the registered

CEO of Yanolja, currently serving as the general CEO, supervising the overall management. The issue is my leadership style.

I thought all I had to do was receive investments, hire talent, provide a good working environment for employees, set goals, acquire companies to meet those goals, set business indicators accordingly, and make sure I reached the goals. But managing an organization is not that simple. Why didn't I realize until now that not everyone shares the same ideas, situation, abilities, or perspective? Or perhaps I already knew all that, but still harboured the illusion that everything would be fine, and things would get done since I have a team of experienced people.

It took time to realize that in an organization, no matter how many people are involved, nothing happens automatically. Since receiving investments as a unicorn company valued at $1 billion in 2019, I have focused my time on acquiring companies, setting goals that align with our strategy, making management decisions and overseeing the general direction, rather than engaging in external activities or promoting brand awareness.

Many new executives have joined, and I believed we were on the right track, thinking that things were going well despite our differing interests. This led to my illusion that everything was running smoothly, based solely on business meetings with management, without thoroughly checking and monitoring the middle and lower levels of the organization. As a result, I only understood internal feelings through reports and documents. I was not sharing or even in touch with our organization's philosophy, motivation, and vision.

Of course, the COVID-19 pandemic and the shift to working from home coincided with this time. In 2022, I found myself deeply engaged in personal self-reproach regarding the situation. Although some of my businesses are experiencing stagnation, the company's overall indicators are growing. And the company is consistently moving toward globalization. However, I know, as do the members of my organization, that if things continue as they are, we risk becoming a company that slows down instead of achieving what we aim for.

Yanolja comprises numerous companies, including Yanolja Service, which is the Yanolja platform; Interpark, which we acquired; Triple, which has merged with Interpark; Yanolja Cloud, a hotel operation solution serving over 180 countries in more than 60 languages, and others.

But when asked, "Are we doing well?" I hesitate to answer, "Yes, we are." You might ask, "Isn't growth all that matters?" or "Can't you keep expanding the business?" But we are still far from perfect. When asked, "Do you sincerely care about your customers?" I find myself embarrassed to confidently say, "Yes, I do." That's when my self-reproach began.

I pondered deeply on the meaning of our existence, which is more important than just keeping our organization moving forward. I realize that even if I manage to keep going and growing, I might find myself in an endless, long tunnel. I recognized what I had to do: set the stage to ensure an environment where we can all focus on what we need to start.

We, not just I, must change. We must follow 'our' voice, instead of 'my' voice, as we work together to find solutions, design the future and act. Relying solely on the boss for these tasks often leads to incorrect answers and represents only a one-sided perspective. Everyone must understand the direction in which we need to go and continually immerse ourselves in creating something that approaches the right answer.

Only then can everyone thrive. It's not until now that I've started to realize that suppliers, users, platforms and members are connected as one. I am just one element in that connection. My opinion is the same: it's just one element. So, I played the card labelled 'Restart Again.'

My motto when I was young was 'Do your best before you regret.' I've reached this point since my 20s by constantly promising myself, "Just refuse to give up until the end." And now, I am pondering immersion. What should I immerse myself in? And what should we immerse ourselves in to make the value of our existence shine most brilliantly? Just because the sun reaches the celestial longitude of 315° doesn't mean that spring has arrived. But there eventually comes a moment when you realize, "It's spring!" without being told or needing to be convinced. I cannot declare this as the time for us to immerse. But I believe that once a path is opened for us to willingly participate, and if we take this path together while constantly checking our sustainable direction, there will come a day when we all realize, "It's spring!" in this new beginning.

The *Restart* of 2015 has already passed through spring, summer and fall, and has now become winter.

And once again, it heralds a new beginning for us. It won't take long this time. I've experienced the laws of compound interest and acceleration.

Now, all I have to do is hold down the right arrow key.

DREAMING OF SUSTAINABLE GROWTH
FOR ALL YANOLJA PEOPLE

I always feel lonely, even as I keep moving forward and the company continues to grow. Over the last 18 years, many employees have joined and left Yanolja. I sincerely hope that they are all growing. Today, I think about and miss the particular friends who started the business with me, with nothing but bare fists in the early days.

Seong-il and Seong-guk were friends who took charge of running the southern branch when we started the business with almost nothing. It's already been over 17 years since we started the business and were forced to pay a security deposit of $5,000 out of concern that we might not earn any money, fail in our business, and end up running away.

Bong-gil was a friend who came to join the company when he was a junior in college. I vividly remember how he hesitated upon seeing our small office, wondering if there was a future for him in this business. His parents thought he was studying in college, but instead, he was doing work unrelated to his major, sitting at a desk in the corner of an officetel.

Jong-gyu, joined the company as a developer after I persuaded him, at a time when we had no developers on the team. And Sang-gyu, who founded the business with me and is still here.

Today, I especially remember the friends with whom I worked for a long time, building Yanolja from the ground up. I am grateful to all the Yanolja people who worked with such passion.

On days like today, I miss them and feel even more thankful. I believe that the company wouldn't be what it is today without their youthful devotion. I sincerely thank them for the time they devoted to the company, which helped Yanolja become a beacon for society and as we continue to grow into the future.

I look forward to seeing all Yanolja people continue to grow in their roles, and I too will challenge myself with all my heart.

March 1, 2023, late at night on the 18th anniversary of Yanolja

CHAPTER 2

READY!

1978–1997

CHILDHOOD

I WAS TRULY PESSIMISTIC
ABOUT THE WORLD

My parents had one son and three daughters, and I was their third child. Under the Confucian culture, which ideologizes and prefers boys, I might have monopolized the love of my parents and older sisters. However, I can only imagine what it was like when I was a toddler, because my father died when I was four years old. As a child, I thought he had died in an accident. It was only after I grew up that I learned from my aunt that my father had committed suicide for some unknown reason by consuming pesticide.

I would be truly grateful if I could live with even a faint memory of my father, but I have no memory of him at all. When I was six, my mother remarried and left the family. I had to live with my grandmother, which, at the time, I didn't think was a big deal. Besides, I was just a little child with no concept of what was normal. Being under my grandmother's care, I didn't have to study. From the second grade of elementary school, I helped my grandmother and uncle pick peppers and even farmed rice. My eldest daughter is in the second grade now, and looking at her, I cannot believe I did that at her age. But back then, even my friends believed it was the natural thing to do if you were born into a farmer's family.

Being raised by my grandmother, I didn't learn how to read and write until I was in the fifth grade. In elementary school, I was seen as a child who didn't do homework, a poor student with low grades and no parents. As a result, emotions other than joy began to take root in my heart. I was always conscious of other people's gazes, and my mind was dominated by resentment toward life.

As time went by, my sense of inferiority toward the world intensified. I hated when people expressed pity for me. Whenever others around me talked about my parents, I became upset and kept silent. Even now, as I write this, I feel sorry for myself because even though I am a parent who loves and raises my own children, I grew up without ever being loved by my parents and have no memories of them.

I learned to read and write thanks to a teacher who was committed to my education. In the sixth grade, while delivering newspapers on a motorcycle, a college student, who was also a newspaper delivery person in the same area, gave me free tutoring. Thanks to him, my grades during junior high improved so much that I moved from the bottom to the middle of the class. Back then, I hated my life so much and harboured nothing but resentment. I resented my father, my mother and my environment. In adulthood, I no longer harboured such resentments, probably because I had exhausted all my resentment in those earlier years.

My nickname was 'Jjanji' (translated as 'Salty Pickle') because my lunch box always contained only kimchi or pickles as a side dish. Fortunately, my friends didn't shun me; they always hung out with me and offered comfort. Perhaps, next to my grandmother, they understood best what I was going through at that time.

My grandmother was the most precious person in my life. But, as fate would have it, she passed away from stomach cancer during winter vacation when I was a freshman in junior high. How could the heavens be so cruel to me? She was like a god who took me under her wings, caring for me in my parents' stead. It seemed unbearably cruel that she was taken from me so early as well.

I was truly pessimistic about the world. At such a young age, shouldn't there have been at least one person I liked and could lean on for solace? It was devastating. For a while, I was in a daze, unable to cope, and I even contemplated ending my life, thinking I had nothing to live for.

People say humans are creatures of adaptation. As the years passed, I found myself living day by day, dominated more by self-pity than thoughts of my grandmother. As a result, I became too busy to harbour resentment toward anyone. Living with my uncle, I had to cook, do laundry, clean the house, and do farm work, all while being a student. Thanks to that, I can now cook delicious food with ease. Fortunately, my middle school grades continued to improve, thanks to the college student who tutored me for free while I was delivering newspapers. Financial constraints led me to choose a vocational high school, but I think I adjusted well. I got good grades in both practical work and classes and acquired certificates faster than others.

Recognizing that I was struggling financially, my school provided me with scholarships, and I was also the first to receive rice during the school's rice drive for poor families. Even now, there is a picture of me receiving the rice donation hanging in the hallway of my high school teachers' lounge, and the look on my face shows how embarrassed I was. Thinking back now, it still brings a smile to my face. Back then, all I could think of was the embarrassment. I didn't think about what I wanted to become. I spent every day earning certifications or doing practical training, but I couldn't envision my future.

After graduating from high school, I found a job, and while working, I noticed the gap between high school and college graduates, which led me to decide to attend college. I studied for a short period to pass a college entrance exam, but with my poor CSAT score, I ended up being admitted to Cheonan Technical College based on my school grades. What I had learned during my three years of high school had a preparatory effect, so the classes were easy, except for the liberal arts subjects. My college life seemed smooth from the outside, but inside, I was increasingly exhausted due to anxiety about the future and financial difficulties.

Not having money means you have to earn money to survive. To earn money, I worked as a construction worker during the school year , and during vacations, I took jobs at construction sites, doing menial labour for room and board. In this way, my college life instilled in me a sense of urgency about money. I started looking for a job by taking advantage of the defense industry's special military service exemption program and ended up getting a job at a defense company before graduation. I began my job with the military service exemption benefit, working in product design, moulding and quality control. In this way, I started working earlier than my peers.

I had not yet turned 20 when I moved to Seoul.

1997–2001

MILITARY SERVICE EXEMPTION

LIFE HAD A TURN OF LUCK IN STORE FOR ME

I came to Seoul in October 1997 after securing a job in the city. This was shortly before the Asian financial crisis, commonly referred to as the 'IMF crisis,' which transpired in November 1997. Then I found out that I had to graduate from college first to be eligible for the military service exemption, as it wasn't legal to receive it while being an enrolled student. So, it was agreed that my military service exemption period would start from March 1998, when I was hired for a design drawing position.

I was full of dreams. It was my first real job, and it felt like a dream come true to be assigned to the drawing development department and receive a special exemption benefit from military service. It was also a dream for a country boy like me to have a life in Seoul. I was paid $600 per month, which made living on my own difficult. Therefore, I decided to commute from my aunt's house, who took pity on me for growing up without parents and had always been kind to me.

I lived at my aunt's house for almost four years, commuting to and from work, even though I was a grown-up who should have been independent. But it didn't bother me much, probably because all I cared about at the time was making and saving money. Yet, I cannot deny there were some inconvenient aspects to this arrangement. Despite these, I lived at my aunt's house while working. I came to Seoul full of dreams and started working at my first job, but most job assignments involved making copies or assembling and delivering lighting samples to be presented to buyers overseas. During technical high school, I studied drafting for three years, and design for two years in college. I got my license and took the job; the pay wasn't bad, considering it was a position I took to get the military service exemption benefit (usually, the monthly salary in such cases was around $400). Since the lighting supplied to US buyers had to pass a safety test, I was tasked with translating the UL (Underwriters Labouratories) standards booklet, which contains the appropriate design standards. As a new hire, I did not realize how important it was to translate the UL standard booklet. At that time, I had such a hard time translating the book with my poor English skills that, by the time I was done, I had memorized the specifications and understood all the terms. The experience made me capable of designing and testing products. Looking back now, it was preparation for my future work. But at the time, I was under the mistaken belief that just being able to draw would solve everything and show my competence.

Being a graduate from a technical high school and an engineering college, my English skills were barely above beginner's level. Despite my best efforts, I struggled to translate even one page of the book in an entire day. Back in 1997, there were no apps for easy translation. I had to search dictionaries or the internet every time I encountered an unknown word. This reality was far from the dreams I had harboured about moving to Seoul, excited to have found a job while still a college student. My sense of value seemed to be diminishing, and I felt like I was constantly walking on eggshells. I felt so out of place and vulnerable, doubting my own capabilities.

I had never smoked, but for the first time, I bought a pack of cigarettes and smoked in secret in the men's restroom. I don't smoke anymore, but that experience shows the extent of the stress I felt while living in Seoul.

Not being able to do anything meaningful made me feel like it wasn't the right place for me. In such a place, you lose your freedom, and your self-esteem hits rock bottom, leaving you feeling miserable. Tasked with work I hated, I often found myself dozing off. A month passed, and there was a company dinner. I didn't have a high alcohol tolerance, but I drank more than I should have and, when I sobered up, I realized I was back home.

It was past eight o'clock in the morning. I was supposed to be at work by nine o'clock, but I was already late. The commute from Sillim-dong to the company at the intersection in front of the Gangsegu Office took an hour by bus and 50 minutes by subway. Taking a taxi was not an option I could afford, so I did my best to get to work using public transport. Feeling guilty for being late, I stole glances to see if my boss was upset, and I sensed that something was amiss. Next to the development room was a room where we made and tested samples. A senior colleague who looked after me called me over and asked, "Do you remember what happened last night?" And then he told me everything I did the night before.

I panicked. How could I have been so irresponsible? I wasn't a heavy drinker, but at the dinner, I drank until I completely passed out. It was a miracle that I even made it home. I wish I had never found out what had happened. The chairman of the company, who was over 70 at the time, called for me.

The company had 20 to 30 employees at its Seoul office and around 70 at its Asan factory. It was a company that exported lighting to the United States and Canada through OEM (Original Equipment Manufacturing). Unlike other companies, it was thriving during the Asian financial crisis. The value of the won plummeted from ₩700 to $1 to over ₩1,400. For exporting companies, this meant they were earning a lot more per product: they received ₩1,400 per dollar, instead of ₩700, effectively increasing their surplus from 10% to 110%.

This was the situation when the chairman called. Was he about to fire me? But why would he call me to his office instead of having a manager or the president handle it? I was panicking as I walked into the chairman's office. However, upon entering, the chairman asked, "Mr. Lee, I need you to draw something on the computer. Is one hour enough?" I responded, "Of course, sir."

When I was in technical high school, computer-aided design (CAD) was introduced to Korea for the first time. I learned on the test version and got certified. Over time, everything transitioned to CAD. At college, there was no one proficient in CAD, so I handled the CAD work and printed it for presentations in the mould department, which proved very useful. At work, drawings were typically sent and received by fax, and the trade department had to constantly explain dimensions and shapes over the phone, which was exhausting. Therefore, creating a drawing in CAD and sending it by email was a groundbreaking innovation.

According to a senior colleague, I had drunkenly voiced my frustrations at the company dinner. I complained that, despite having a certificate in computer drawing and my background in high school and college focusing on drawing, products and moulds, nobody in the company was effectively utilizing my skills. I was told to go home, but I didn't and kept lamenting how difficult work was because no one asked me to do what I excelled at. The chairman witnessed all of this, and that's how I got my first real assignment.

The incident turned out to be a stroke of luck, but as a newly-hired young man of about 20 who had caused a drunken scene, I was so embarrassed. For a while, I couldn't keep my head up. After the incident, I was tasked with using the company's CAD program to convert all manual drawings into computerized ones. At a young age, I began to earn the company's trust in areas such as product design, quality, bias pack management and moulds.

This trust was fully reflected in my salary, and by the time my special military service exemption period ended, my annual salary had exceeded $20,000. It was a salary level nearly impossible for an industrial technical worker hired for the special military service exemption benefit.

FORTUNATELY, I KEPT AIMING HIGHER

The world was not easy. At a young age, I should have been content with my work, but as my salary increased and I became accustomed to living in Seoul, I aspired to become even wealthier. In Seoul, it seemed there were only two options: to live in poverty or in wealth. I entrusted my salary to a trust savings account with Hanmi Bank. It was a regular deposit account but it did not protect the principal. The interest rate on this account was variable but high, averaging between 13 to 15 percent annually.

It may be hard to believe now, but during the Asian financial crisis, interest rates were unusually high. This fuelled my determination to become rich, and from then on, whenever I had free time, I frequented bookstores, devouring self-help books, books on economics and stocks, real estate,and auctions. I discovered a few books that became treasures to me, including *Rich Dad, Poor Dad* and *Who Moved My Cheese?*

The company continued to thrive due to strong exports. The chairman sold the company to an American firm, making a profit while continuing to work as CEO. However, the company faced difficulties in the month when salaries were supposed to be adjusted. Not a single person defended the company, and gossip about it intensified with each passing day. This had been a recurring issue every year, leading to divisions among the employees. Amid this turmoil, I often imagined that if I were to start a company, I would strive not to be a business owner who was constantly subject to gossip and criticism.

But the world is not that easy. Now that I am a business owner, I realize that reality is not as simple as it seemed. However, the good news is that I am still aiming higher. That's why I left the company that had trusted me and offered me so much, driven by my determination to become wealthy. I wanted to become truly rich, not live like a hamster running endlessly on a treadmill. *Rich Dad, Poor Dad* gave me the definition of true wealth, and *Who Moved My Cheese?* taught me not to be complacent. Since moving to Seoul at the young age of 20 and living at my aunt's house, I've experienced many ups and downs. But whenever possible, I kept books with me that I believed would help me become wealthy while saving money.

That period in my life marked the end of illusions I'd had about the world since my college days, as I confronted reality and began to dream of wealth. Had my company gone bankrupt and had I enlisted like my friends during the Asian financial crisis, life would have been very different. Fortunately, I was lucky enough to work for a thriving export company. I saw this as the first step in my adult life, living by my own will, and felt it was time to stand on my own two feet. Perhaps my eagerness to make money faster and easier stemmed from my determination to be independent. At that time, I was captivated by many fanciful ideas about easy money-making and ended up investing in stocks. This led to some devastating experiences while still working for the company, but it marked the beginning of my unforgettable journey into youth and adulthood.

2001-2005

YEARS I WORKED AS A MOTEL JANITOR

A LIFETIME'S WORTH OF FAILURES
ALL AT ONCE

I left the company after about three and a half years, at the age of 23. Despite my youth, I felt a sense of helplessness, having lost $20,000 out of the $40,000 I had saved while working at the company, all due to stock investments. In *Rich Dad, Poor Dad*, the author emphasized that wealth begins with saving seed money, but instead, I found myself depleting my funds.

The decision to leave the company was driven by my dream of becoming a full-time investor, which led me to enroll in a stock investment school. However, the more I learned about stock investment, the more my bank balance dwindled. While working at the company, I convinced myself I was investing with a long-term view, but when stock prices fell, my patience wore thin, and I sold my stocks in haste. This cycle continued, and as I attended the school, I fell into the pitfall of ultra-short-term trading, more often losing money than making any. My future became increasingly uncertain.

Fortunately, I found some freelance drawing opportunities. However, my focus was divided, and my mind was cluttered. After much deliberation, I decided to quit stock investing and began contemplating my next steps. During this time, I discovered online that working as a motel janitor could earn me more than $2,500 a month, with free room and board included.

I inquired about the job and learned that I would be provided with a room where I could stay warm in winter and cool in summer, in addition to meals. After much thought, I decided to accept it. I reasoned that if I had been able to save $40,000 by saving wages for three and a half years at my previous company, I could manage this job too. The stock investment had been my first major failure in life. I had done drawing for a living, briefly engaged in day-trading, and now I was about to start a new chapter as a motel janitor. However, the job was not as straightforward as I had thought. I was instructed to bring nothing but underwear, sportswear, and slippers in my bag, and I couldn't be sure that the job was legitimate. Although I was determined to take the job, I became fearful. I called my close friends and asked them to report to the police if they lost contact with me before I started cleaning a motel located in Sindorim.

I had quit my job as spring arrived, spent the summer fiercely engaging in stock investments, and by winter, I found myself cleaning a motel. That's how I spent the difficult year of 2001. The motel cleaning job was far from easy. My day began with changing bed sheets at 10 am and didn't end until midnight. By the time I had finished sorting recycling and garbage, it was often past 1 am.

I was exhausted, yet I couldn't easily fall asleep. I felt a sense of sadness, questioning whether I was on the right path. My life seemed incredibly bleak, and this feeling weighed heavily on me every night as I went to bed. While working as a motel janitor, I learned about the motel business and eventually took on the position of assistant motel manager. This role, positioned between the manager and the cleaner, involved parking assistance, front cashier support, managing guest rooms, room service, and virtually everything else required to run a motel business.

You could say it was like an assistant manager's role in general companies, typically involving the most groundwork and legwork. The salary was about $2,000 a month, with a rotation of 24 hours on followed by 24 hours off. Since the lodging industry operates 365 days a year, it must always be open and ready to receive guests. Therefore, staff must always be present, and if someone misses a shift, someone else must cover it.

The challenge was more about having to be at work for 24 hours rather than the physical labour itself. I would finish my shift at 10 am, take a shower, and sleep deeply. In the evening, I would wake up, have dinner, and often enjoy a bottle of beer on the rooftop above my room, gazing at the lights between the buildings. It was sad to realize that none of those countless lights belonged to me.

Up until then, I had been diligently saving money, but in fact, I had temporarily forgotten the lessons I'd learned from *Rich Dad, Poor Dad*. It seemed like I was in a daze, focused solely on saving money. Of course, I continued to read finance-themed books and pondered ways to become wealthy, but the idea of being truly rich seemed like a dream that had faded away.

I longed for my own light. I aspired to someday own a motel and to have a comfortable place to live. Since childhood, I never really had a home – a place I could call my own. In moments that I contemplated when I would emerge from this long tunnel and live as an independent man, the future appeared grim. I found myself engulfed in depression, questioning whether I could ever achieve what I wanted, rather than nurturing positive thoughts. Nonetheless, I tried to appear confident to others. I intentionally greeted people louder than necessary and performed my work energetically, pretending that nothing was too challenging.

However, I made a point not to make eye contact with customers while providing service. The customer was king, and the more I treated them like royalty, the more tips I received. But internally, I was constantly consumed by self-doubt, wondering how long I would have to live this way.

A year and a half later, having saved enough seed money, I found myself planning a business. I think it was the only time I truly smiled, happy with my idea. After visiting a nameless salad factory in Daejeon, I hastily decided to start a salad business. But that venture was just a fantasy. I learned the hard lesson that starting a business without proper preparation is likely to fail, and once again, I lost the seed money I had saved. It doesn't seem like a lot of money, but at the time, it was precious, saved over two years. My short six-month venture into the salad business brought me back to square one.

I was faced with the decision to return to drawing, literally and figuratively, or to work as a motel manager. I chose the latter because the pay was good. I then opened an online community on Daum to share information among motel workers. The community gradually grew, eventually reaching nearly 10,000 members.

While working as a motel manager, I began to draft a business plan. In the end, I revisited my old books. During this time, I realized there was a lesson missing in *Rich Dad, Poor Dad* and *Who Moved My Cheese?* The books taught me the importance of saving seed money, but they didn't emphasize the importance of starting with something I knew best and could do best.

When I started the salad business, I jumped in without knowing much about salads. My ignorance led me to assess the business's feasibility solely through internet searches. At the same time, I was the kind of person who, despite being young, prided himself on being 'smart' by reading various economic books, self-help books and guides on writing business plans.

But I knew I couldn't work as a motel manager indefinitely. I began to ponder my next steps. Many people visited the online community for motel workers and sent me numerous promotional inquiries. While I hadn't been in the business for long, my experience in the industry and success in running the online community set me apart. Using the online community of motel workers as a model, I created a website to promote motel suppliers. I planned a business offering comparative pricing and comprehensive information.

After concluding my second unsuccessful business, serving salads, I embarked on my third entrepreneurial challenge. I spent over a year preparing for this new venture, finding investors and partners who were interested in starting a business with me, including the current Yanolja Vice President and CEO of Yanolja F&G, a small and medium-sized hotel franchise, Im Sang-gyu. I began preparations in the summer of 2004, and the business officially launched in March 2005 under the name 'Hotel Motel Pension' as an individual, simplified taxpayer.

I had the experience of working in a motel, starting as a cleaner and progressing to a motel manager, then to a general manager. I was proud of myself. My investors, too, had been in the motel business for over ten years.

I was confident, with a solid business plan, job experience, knowledge of the system and more. The online community for motel workers had grown to over 10,000 members, and it seemed like I had everything needed for a successful business. I saw this as an opportunity to achieve all that I ever wanted: my own place in the city and to own a motel, ending the pity I felt as a motel cleaner and the helplessness I experienced after the failed salad business, which led me to consider ending my life.

Wise men say that failure is the mother of success and that hard times are a process for greater growth. I was sure that no more hard times would come my way. I was complacent, thinking that my share of hardships in childhood and youth was enough. I was that confident. Little did I know, I was rushing toward my third failure.

My life as a motel worker came to an end after four and a half years. I quit my job at a hotel in Uijeongbu, Gyeonggi Province, which served as an accommodation for US soldiers and some Koreans and started my own business in an apartment in Uijeongbu that belonged to one of my investors.

CHAPTER 3

START!

2005

FIRST YEAR
SINCE FOUNDING

THE FUTURE WAS UNCERTAIN,
BUT I MADE A START AND PROGRESSED

I began earnestly planning my business about a year before I quit my job in the motel business. I presented my business plan to acquaintances, asking for their opinions on its potential success and inquiring if they were interested in investing. I also managed to impress a small group of about 30 members from the online community of motel workers. In today's terms, these were my Investor Relations (IR) activities. With only a few pages of a business plan, I persuaded them to invest and participate in my venture. Out of all the people I approached, a friend in the motel and cafe business decided to invest. This group also included the manager of the motel where I had previously worked, the sales director of the hotel in Uijeongbu where I was employed just before starting my business, and the current vice president of Yanolja, who was in the same tennis club as me in college and had started working at a motel after consulting with me. Our team of five founded a company named Hotel Motel Pension with $50,000 in capital. We began drafting business plans in the summer of 2004. Together, we built a website, held occasional meetings, and discussed our direction and financial plans. Through this process, we became a close-knit team, harbouring the illusion that everything would go well in the future.

I had two failures in my life: one in stock investment and the other in the salad business. Therefore, I thought I should at least try a third time. This time, I felt a secret reassurance because the company was founded by people from the motel industry, and all the conditions seemed right for success. We started the company in March 2005 when the website was somewhat complete. We spent our days eagerly anticipating the launch of the website. To save funds, one of the investors allowed us to use their apartment as an office, where the current Vice President of Yanolja and I started the business with just two desks. The other investors continued with their regular jobs.

Since the startup team consisted only of the current Yanolja Vice President and myself, we began searching for more people. As an online company, our priority was to find a designer, but it was challenging.

If we could have offered good benefits, the situation might have been better. However, we could only offer a small salary, and our business direction was not yet clear. Moreover, it was related to the motel business, which was not particularly appealing. Eventually, we conducted interviews in a nearby cafe instead of the apartment, managing to hire a designer and someone for sales. With the website nearing completion, our spirits were soaring high.

However, what I didn't realize was that the $50,000 capital would quickly vanish once we started paying wages to employees and the website design company we had outsourced. It was just enough to cover six months of business operations, and I naively started the business with the plan to work hard in marketing and sales for six months, then start generating profits and stabilizing the business. But the money disappeared faster than we anticipated.

To cut costs, we bought groceries from a nearby market and cooked our own lunches. We never went out for company dinners. Despite our scrambling, no sales came in. Eventually, it was agreed that the investors would invest additional amounts each month according to their share percentages. There was no end in sight to our deficit streak.

We were running the business with impractical strategies, such as collecting advertising fees from motel supply companies. We believed we had a good channel to promote our business to motel owners, given the large number of members in our online community. However, these ideas failed, and our B2B venture started to seem hopeless. As the business continued, more people, including the head of a web agency, joined the company. Despite these additions, our financial situation went from bad to worse.

The future seemed so uncertain, but I couldn't stop. My drive wasn't so much due to the fear of returning to a life as a motel cleaner, but rather the dread of having to reset my future and start from scratch, potentially being labelled a failure for the rest of my life. The business was also struggling internally, as around that time one of the investors, a friend of mine who was an administrator of our Daum Cafe online community, left the company.

Meanwhile, I was contacted by the creator of 'Motel Tour,' a Daum community with 10,000 members. It was a community of motel users, and the creator wanted me to take it over. I accepted his proposal immediately. At the time, the largest online community of motel users was 'Motel Guide,' boasting 70,000 members with significant influence. 'Motel Tour' was the third largest, but I intuitively felt it presented another challenge and opportunity. I acquired 'Motel Tour' for about $5,000 and dedicated myself to it day and night.

I typically left Uijeongbu at 10 am for field sales, and it was often 3 or 4 am before I returned to our office-cum-accommodation apartment. I had to stay out that late because motel managers usually finished their shifts at midnight, and that was the only time I could talk and have drinks with them. By day, I worked in advertising sales; by night, I was out building a network. My weight, which was initially 150 lbs, ballooned to 190 lbs a year after starting my business.

Just because I was working hard didn't mean the company was making a profit. Payday always made me nervous, but I consistently wire-transferred salaries between the third and ninth of each month, even though employees were supposed to be paid on the tenth of the following month. I never paid them late. I believe that's the minimum promise a business should keep with its employees. Their salaries were my priority. I might have been late on other bills, but I always paid the employees first, which then brought me peace of mind. My salary was set at $500 and the vice president's at $700, but I never took my full salary.

I often found myself needing to source funds from elsewhere to contribute my share of capital to the company, instead of drawing a salary from it. The vice president even sold his car to cover expenses. During the business planning stage, I had made financial plans, but they never worked out. The expenses were double what I had anticipated, and sales were half what we expected. I kept ignorantly running the business, persevering day after day, thinking that since I was young, passionate, always hungry, and would not give up, that someday I would succeed. However, business isn't something one can start just by recklessly jotting down plans.

In business, you may have a great plan, but it's merely a vision or wish for the future. Reality doesn't always align with your plan. For me, the most challenging aspect of running a business was always managing cash flow. The more I chased money, the more elusive it seemed. It appears that understanding and adapting to change is crucial in business. It's a mysterious factor that determines whether you can find a growth engine, depending on how quickly you recognize reality and adjust your strategies and indicators. Even now, still in business, it feels the same. Perhaps I didn't just start a business; I embarked on a journey to gradually understand money and people.

LET TODAY BE THE DAY
I'LL MISS TOMORROW

For a moment, I think of a hyena searching for food. I'm trying to find some time to relax because, with a long way still to go, I'm beginning to feel a bit impatient. I believe that by addressing things one at a time, good days will eventually come. There will be a day in the not-too-distant future when I will look back on today with fondness and nostalgia, recognizing it as a good memory.

It wasn't a hard day. What is difficult is the feeling of emptiness inside, and the self-reproach about my business methods and the actions I take while running around. But I know this: I have the strength to handle the situation and achieve something. That's who I am. Success lies beyond this challenge.

Let's not be afraid!

Don't be lazy! Always work hard!

Sujin Lee, you worked hard today. Tomorrow, strive to soar even higher.

August 19, 2005, 00:45

I'M EXCITED AS I STAND ON
THE CUSP OF A NEW DAY

Today, I went out to work at 1:00 pm and returned home at 5:00 am. It's a strange feeling. It's like I've been in a well all this time, and yet, it feels like I've discovered another side of myself. There's no fatigue, only joy in the work. Joy is a great teacher, guiding me toward what to do next. I'll make a promise to myself: I will ensure that I do my best for as long as I can in what I love doing. I've finished today's work, and soon, I'll start another day's work. I am filled with excitement as I stand at the threshold of a new day.

That's our approach to doing business.

August 23, 2005, 05:59

I AM HAPPIEST BECAUSE IT'S
THE HARDEST

Marriage problems, money problems. In some ways, today is my most difficult time, as my heart feels emptier than ever before. But I know that this period will be remembered as the happiest time in my life, because I have never run as hard as I am now. I have never thought as deeply as I do now. It's hard, but I'm happy.

August 30, 2005, 00:57

SOMETIMES YOU JUST HAVE TO GO THROUGH A LONG TUNNEL

These days, I feel as if something is visible and within my reach, only to disappear. It feels like I'm passing through a long tunnel. If you pass through a tunnel this long, you should eventually reach a place where people live, but the tunnel seems long and endless.

September 9, 2005

LET'S GIVE FIRST AND LEAVE THEM WITH NO CHOICE BUT TO ACKNOWLEDGE IT

Am I just complaining? The more I think about it, the more it seems that I have nothing but complaints. Am I anxious while working, even though I told myself to be happy in my work? If so, I am far from the path to success. Let's think, always. Let's try not to think of receiving first. Let others acknowledge: they cannot do without me, without my company.

When that happens, the value of this company will rise significantly. However, doing nothing now and merely asking for a value increase is a strategy that won't work for anyone. Let's always give first. Let's promote motels first, help them get lots of orders first. And let's always be happy, including myself as I guide them, telling them they can be happy too. That's what I should do. If I'm full of complaints and anxiety while doing business, failure is inevitable. Success comes only with joy and happiness, and not just mine, but also my clients'.

October 30, 2005, 14:01

2006

SECOND YEAR
SINCE FOUNDING

JUST REFUSE TO GIVE UP UNTIL THE END

"I refuse to give up until the end."

This mantra, etched in my mind and heart, has become the motto of my life, my personal code of conduct. It represents my values that are essential for living a life without regrets, regardless of what I create or the results I achieve. If I approach something half-heartedly and carelessly, only to claim, "I worked hard. This is all that can be done," what meaningful changes can be expected in our words, actions and hearts?

Anyone can think. Anyone can decide and start acting. However, the law of the world dictates that not everyone will enjoy favourable results. I believe the difference lies not in drawing a line, being satisfied and rationalizing, but in refusing to give up until the very end. A good result does not necessarily equate a successful one. You may fail and not achieve favourable outcomes now, but the extent of patience, thought and repeated effort you put into the process determines your ability to find solutions in the future. This approach reduces the probability of failure. I believe this approach brings you one step closer to living your own, authentic life.

When I first started Yanolja, I personally handled sales. Our initial business model was an online community called Daum Café, which promoted motels. To keep the company afloat, I had to visit motel owners, pitch our services and secure advertising orders. Although had about five salespeople, none were producing significant results. Consequently, as the president of the company, I had to step in and take charge of sales myself. I remember visiting every motel, meeting with employees, managers and owners, and pitching Yanolja until my mouth ran dry, ensuring no motel was left unvisited. Now that Yanolja has become somewhat established, 'advertising a motel' seems like a routine, everyday concept. However, in the early days, the idea of motel advertising as a business model was unheard of in Korea. This meant I was presenting a novel idea to people who had never even considered advertising their businesses.

When I proposed advertising their motels, the usual response was, "Why bother to advertise my motel? Why is it necessary?" If I suggested, "You will get a lot more customers," they would retort, "I already have plenty of customers without advertising. Why should I spend money and even offer discounts?" As the president, I didn't have a convincing answer to that question, which made me wonder how our sales staff must have felt. The motel owners, already enjoying plenty of business, were being approached by our sales staff who were asking them to pay for monthly advertisements and offer discounts or special service hours to Yanolja members. To them, this proposal was nonsensical. Imagine a popular restaurant where customers must wait at least 30 minutes for a table. If you brought a camera and offered to advertise the restaurant, only to be told not to take photos, how would you react? And if a newly established company specializing in restaurant advertising approached them saying, "Advertise with us, and give a 10% discount to customers who find your restaurant through our website," what would the restaurant owner's reaction be? That was precisely the situation we were in.

Should I abandon the business concept of advertising motels? The situation was concerning. I felt devastated when suspicions arose about me being a fraud. Understandably, I might not have appeared convincing. Here I was, a young fellow of plain appearance, claiming to be the president of a company, driving an old car, and proposing to promote their business for a monthly fee ranging from $150 to $1,000. It was upsetting and depressing, but I was determined not to stop. My years of field experience convinced me that Yanolja had significant potential as a business model. I visited and met with motel employees, managers, and owners, facing rejection time and again, yet I never thought of quitting, despite burning through money on maintenance and gas for my 1994 Accent. Then, a turning point arrived. One day, a motel owner mentioned, "Things haven't been consistent lately."

"What do you mean?" I asked.

"In the past, guests just kept walking in, but lately, business has sometimes been slow."

That was my "Aha!" moment. I suggested to the owner, "Think of this marketing as insurance. Give it a try, like you're signing up for insurance. I'll strive to eliminate your slow days. If you trust me as your future insurance, I promise you'll gain much more than what you'd pay for in insurance."

In the end, I managed to sell the most expensive advertisement banner for $1,000. That was the day I secured my first motel advertisement and the same day my company landed our inaugural motel ad. Over several years, I maintained a close relationship with the motel owner, who would consult with me about any issues at the motel. He even confided in me about his personal problems and often expressed his gratitude by taking me out for meals.

Attending his funeral, I was overwhelmed with sadness, especially recalling the day he placed his first order with me. He was the one who trusted me as his insurance, supported me passionately, and understood me deeply. To me, he was an incredibly precious person. I often ponder whether Yanolja would have reached its current success if I had tried to find solutions only in my head, saving on gas, or if I had decided to quit when I couldn't secure any advertisement orders.

I may not be a man of great intellect, but I strive to be a man of action, both physically and mentally. I believe that perseverance, even in the face of trials and failures, turns these experiences into a unique experience that cannot be taken away. This concept of marketing as insurance quickly became the driving force behind securing over 50 advertisements. This momentum was built from the know-how I gained and my commitment to never give up, even after ten months of tireless efforts, numerous setbacks, frustrations and false accusations of fraud.

So, even now, when faced with difficult situations, unexpected troubles or challenges I haven't anticipated, the first thing I remind myself of is, "Just don't give up until the end." Many may see this as a cliché. However, it's common for people to advise others on what to say and do but fail to apply the same standards to themselves. My point is about being true to oneself. It's crucial to reflect on whether you're genuinely doing what you believe you should be doing, rather than judging others. Isn't it more important to spend time introspecting than critiquing others?

Sujin Lee, how about you? Nowadays, you're facing many challenges and have grand goals and visions. Are you confident? Absolutely, I am. I have the confidence to work tirelessly and not give up until the very end. I'll worry about the outcome later.

YANOLJA: A GIFT RECEIVED
AT THE DOOR TO HELL

We faced numerous crises from the outset. In fact, our journey began amid a crisis. Despite burning through capital, we were not generating any sales. Full of ambition when we started, we nonetheless spent over a year in deficit. As an inexperienced company head, I lacked expertise in capital management and crisis handling; my only strategy was to spend money frugally.

The early days of Yanolja mirrored the typical experiences of startups. The first year of business is a challenging period where resilience is the key to survival. Achieving profitability is daunting because running a company involves a multitude of expenses, both small and large. Yanolja, too, experienced monthly losses after settling all bills. During this time, my primary role as CEO was running here and there to secure funding.

Yanolja employees were never paid precisely on payday, yet I initiated wire transfers earlier, whether it was the third, fifth or seventh, whenever I had sufficient funds. This was to ensure payment before the balance potentially dropped below the required amount. I later learned that my employees assumed these early payments indicated the company's good financial health.

In some ways, I must critique myself for not having fully communicated the company's situation to my employees. However, consistently meeting payroll deadlines established a foundation of trust. A company cannot function without trust. In retrospect, prioritizing employee salaries was a wise strategy to navigate the financial crises.

Members of a newly established company often lack the time to focus solely on productive work. However, when faced with a crisis, their ability to commit to other productive tasks is further hindered by the stress of managing the crisis. Therefore, it's crucial to initiate crisis management before any crisis occurs. Without prior preparation, you'll find yourself overwhelmed and unable to take control, akin to being trapped in a prison of worries and escape plans. Regrettably, Yanolja also experienced this kind of unpreparedness and ensuing confusion during a crisis.

At its inception, Yanolja was named Motel Tour, and we used 'MoTu' as an abbreviation for our service. Just when the company began to make steady profits and showed growth potential, we lost the trademark rights to 'Motu' to a competitor, due to our lack of awareness about trademark laws. We had been using this name for a year and a half, and for a company that had built its reputation through web services, being forced to abandon our name and start anew was devastating. We were disoriented and didn't know how to proceed. Our attempts to negotiate with the competitor failed. As a result, we had to set aside our usual productive activities for two to three months and focus solely on resolving this issue. It was an incredibly stressful period for us.

It wasn't until August 2006 that we finally abandoned the 'Motu' trademark and adopted 'Yanolja' instead. Nowadays, many people appreciate the name 'Yanolja,' but at that time, it was an unusual, unheard-of name, and even many within our company were reluctant to use it as our service trademark. In hindsight, that crisis marked a pivotal moment that led to the establishment of the 'Yanolja' brand. However, at the time, everyone was demoralized by the fear that the company might shut down. All this could have been avoided if we had understood the trademark system beforehand. We lost valuable time for growth and endured the hardship of losing our name, all due to our lack of preparation in these fundamental areas.

Predicting the exact nature of a crisis is impossible. The good news, however, is that there are always some signs of an impending crisis, in one form or another, before it strikes. To spot these signs, which are key to overcoming a crisis, one must continually seek knowledge and be observant of their environment. It's crucial to constantly question what the risk factors are and to simulate scenarios to counter them. Understanding world changes and trends is also extremely important.

Continuous efforts in crisis management can significantly reduce the likelihood of a company falling into crisis. Nevertheless, it is nearly impossible for new companies to be fully prepared for a crisis. They often lack the experience to make informed judgments and face limitations in technology and capital. Even their brand awareness is typically low. Startups are in a vulnerable position, as if constantly facing potential crises. However, this should not be cause for discouragement.

No company can achieve robust growth without facing crises. A company's trajectory, whether it declines or grows, depends largely on how well it handles and overcomes these challenges. This was certainly true for Yanolja. Starting with a capital of $50,000 and a small group of individuals, we have faced numerous crises both internally and externally before growing into what we are today. However, my employees and I never lost sight of our goals, turning each crisis into an opportunity. We have grown and matured by overcoming the various challenges and setbacks encountered along the way. There may be even greater challenges ahead than those we have already faced. Yet, as we have always done, we will transform these potential crises into opportunities.

ASKING FOR HELP IS PART OF DOING YOUR BEST

One day, a son was constructing steppingstones using large rocks. He had almost completed the task, with only the last rock left to position. Exhausted and struggling under the weight of the heavy rock, he found it immovable, despite his best efforts and profuse sweating. Observing this, his father approached and encouraged him, "Son, it's tough, but give it your all. You'll manage it more easily."

The son responded, "Father, I'm truly doing my best, but no matter how hard I try, it just won't move. It seems impossible for me to lift this alone."

The father listened and said, "Son, think again: have you really done your absolute best?"

Then, adding his own strength to his son's efforts, they lifted the stone together. Gradually, the immovable stone shifted, and the son was finally able to complete the steppingstones. Upon completion, the father imparted a lesson, "Son, you don't have to do everything by yourself to do your best. I was right here beside you, yet you didn't ask for my help. Without it, you might not have been able to finish this project. Remember, seeking help when you genuinely need it is also a part of doing your best."

Just like in this story, we often mistakenly believe that handling things alone is the best approach. However, collabourating with others can be the most effective strategy, especially when you are exhausted or when greater results can be achieved through joint efforts.

September 19, 2006, 14:09

NOW THAT I'VE STARTED,
I'LL PUSH FORWARD UNTIL THE END

Engaging in a task with no end in sight calls for a strategic approach. Rather than blindly pushing to the end, consider it an opportunity for a fresh start. With the creation of Yanolja's own independent website, a real beginning has emerged. Now that I've started, I'm committed to doing it right and with enthusiasm. My path, once shrouded in fog, is now clear. Let's do this.

November 23, 2006, 00:12

IF YOU DON'T RISE TO THE CHALLENGE, YOU CANNOT GRAB THE OPPORTUNITY

Opportunities continuously present themselves to me. My position requires listening to many stories, making opportunities seem ubiquitous. However, not all opportunities are meant to be pursued. If I tried to seize every single one, I'd be running a general store by now. Success is more likely when focusing on opportunities that align with my values, are enjoyable, match my expertise, and fall within my field of study. Such opportunities warrant full commitment, even when exhausting. Therefore, I must identify opportunities in areas where I excel and have the most knowledge. About five years ago, a former colleague from my motel cleaning days approached me. He said,

"Sujin, please help me find a manager job."

I was surprised. "You've been working at the same motel for eight years and are already recognized as a general manager. Why are you looking to leave?"

He explained why he had to leave his current job. With motel management being his only expertise and as a father needing a stable income, he was seeking another managerial position. He had worked in motels for over ten years, during which time he bought three properties in the Gyeonggi Province area, with the intention of renting them out. I advised him to stop searching for a manager job – it took me two hours to dissuade him. Finding him another managerial position was possible, but how much longer did he plan to live, working 365 days a year without a break? I told him that after over 10 years in the same line of work, it was time to aim higher.

Following our conversation, he sold the apartment he had bought, leased a small 30-room motel in Songdo, Incheon, and became the motel owner. Today, he is the proud owner of his own motel business. Whenever he sees me, he always says,

"I make a good living thanks to you. I owe you a lot. It's scary to think about where I might be if I hadn't seized that opportunity and faced the challenge. I would probably still be a motel manager, constantly worrying about my future."

All I did was offer two hours of persuasion. During that time, I pointed out his unique situation: the ability to sell an apartment to rent a motel, over ten years of hard-earned experience, a strong work ethic and his youth. These factors, I argued, positioned him well to take on new challenges and potentially succeed. Of course, failure was a possibility, but my belief was that if you give your best to what you know best, even if it doesn't result in huge success, at least the problem of making a living would be resolved.

Opportunities are akin to seeds sown in a field. The effectiveness of your farming determines the size of your harvest and acts as a measure of your readiness to face challenges. I also believe that the path to success after accepting a challenge lies within oneself, not in external factors or the economic climate. Thus, I continue to focus on what I excel at and enjoy doing. Sure, it sometimes causes headaches, but I see it as a necessary and fortunate part of my journey. To me, life loses its meaning without challenges. Therefore, seizing opportunities for self-challenge and striving to excel in my work are essential.

2007

THIRD YEAR
SINCE FOUNDING

LET'S QUIETLY THROW A STONE
AT THE CALM DAILY ROUTINE

I'm blazing through life, constantly moving forward without a clear sense of direction or purpose. Occasionally, I pause and reflect, only to feel a sense of pity for myself for relentlessly charging ahead as if there's no tomorrow. I quietly throw a stone into the still waters of my daily routine – challenging the illusion that sheer speed will lead me to my goal, without truly knowing if I'm even on the right path.

When I look back, I ask myself: "Am I on the right path? How far have I come?" I can only be sure I'm headed in the right direction if I maintain the passion I had at the start and continually reassess my goals. When running a business, there are times when I find myself unwittingly caught up in the swift pace of change happening around me.

Ideally, I should navigate these changes with intention, but often, I rush forward, influenced by trends and others' opinions of what's right or wrong. There's still a long road ahead, with many strategies I haven't yet tried. I sometimes realize that I've been inadvertently swept off my course by my eagerness for something new and trendy. That's when I take a moment to pause and look back.

Am I progressing well? It's hard to tell. Since humans cannot foresee the future, we must look back at the path we've travelled to evaluate how earnestly we've followed the right direction, whether we've strayed, or if we're veering toward a wrong turn.

Anyone in business will keep moving forward briskly with their eyes fixed firmly on the ground, then sometimes stop and glance up at the sky, without even realizing it, without anyone pointing it out. It's instinctual. If we trust this instinct and reflect on our own and our company's past, pulling together what has become disordered, we are often reminded of our initial commitment. This helps us reclaim our identity and find the right path.

We sometimes forget who we are, how we have lived, and how we intend to continue living. We make excuses about being too busy, claiming we don't have time to think about it, too preoccupied with handling immediate situations. I am no exception, especially now as the head of a company. Days turn into months, and months into years. While each day might not feel urgent, a whole year can feel incredibly pressing.

Looking back, I've constantly been under pressure, always scrambling to find solutions to problems. But isn't it the nature of business that you must keep resetting your horizons and never stop? However, this doesn't mean one should just keep moving forward without pause. Particularly when encountering obstacles, I prefer to step back and seek insights from past experiences or advice from those around me. Yet, implementing this approach is easier said than done.

In emergency situations, people often act hastily and rashly. They easily lose sight of what needs to be done and what the priorities are. Only after the initial response do they realize there were more options than they initially thought. In essence, the urgency to find a quick solution often overshadows the pursuit of the best solution.

It's essential to be able to step back, reflect on ourselves, take a deep breath for a moment and reassess if we are on the right path. There have been many crises and opportunities, as well as numerous changes and slumps.

Times when everything moved faster than a bullet, and times when it seemed time itself had stopped. Not all those days can be satisfying. Not every moment can work in your favour.

Ultimately, I was faced with the decision to find something that would not only satisfy me and Yanolja but also pave the way for future growth and increased chances of success. Before making that decision, it was crucial to understand the goal I was aiming for and why that particular path was necessary. Perhaps it's time to deeply consider how we can achieve growth in our future value. Therefore, I am taking a moment to pause, look back and hope that the outcome will lay a foundation for our future growth.

CHANGE BEGINS WHEN YOU ARE MADLY IN LOVE WITH SOMETHING

What are our limits? Isn't it our mindset, believing that there's only so much we can do, that creates these limits? I still haven't identified our breaking point.

Reflecting on the present and past, the most disappointing aspect is the lack of passion. For us, passion that knows no bounds is our greatest strength. Passion manifests in actions before it finds its way into words. It's evident in even the simplest activities like brushing your teeth, taking a shower or while trying to sleep. Sometimes, it's only when I see someone transform into a person brimming with a kind of mad intensity that I truly witness passion.

The thrill that comes from discovering something you fall madly in love with is truly amazing. Sometimes, my employees struggle with my intense passion. But I believe that together, we are nurturing values that will flourish in the future. Change begins when you are deeply, passionately in love with something. Let's stop making excuses when faced with the boundaries we've set for ourselves. Once those boundaries are crossed, nothing is too difficult. As long as passion is alive and vibrant, there are no limits.

April 26, 2007, 09:57

WITHOUT CHANGE, YOU STOP GROWING AND EVENTUALLY DIE

Not everything can belong to me. It's only by letting go of what needs to be released that you gain the strength to live. Ownership comes when you, in fact, don't own something. Let's, therefore, abandon the consignment division. It revolves around things I didn't create myself, and clinging to them out of greed only tarnishes my character. If I lose focus, I risk missing out on what could rightfully be mine.

As Yanolja grows, it's essential to accompany this growth with appropriate change. Without it, we risk the absurdity of physical growth without the corresponding expansion in capacity, akin to outgrowing clothes that become too small and uncomfortable. At this juncture, it's crucial to consider what actions to take and how to implement them to make significant progress.

Change needs to start in areas we've only half-heartedly addressed. However, without a proper ethos, attempts to systematize change will fail. It seems the time has come, somewhat prematurely, to navigate through self-right-eousness and hypocrisy, coexistence, and compromise, along with a myriad of emotions and actions. If I once feared this moment, I now see it as a doorway to a signifi-cant leap forward; a chance to upgrade and evolve.

Without change, there is no growth. Whether the issues are visible or invisible yet felt in the heart, they pose a real problem. If unaddressed, these could lead to failure. We must embrace change to continue living and thriving.

August 27, 2007, 02:39

MY LOVED ONES,
MY SOURCE OF COURAGE

It was wonderful to have a company dinner with my employees for the first time in a long while. Perhaps autumn is approaching – I feel a sense of melancholy. It's been incredibly hot, but now the air is cool and fresh, typical of autumn weather. I should take my employees out to dinner more often and listen to their stories, but our hectic schedule has made this difficult until tonight. Reflecting on the past and looking to the future is part of my daily routine, and I'm grateful to have people who are reliable indicators and companions on my journey.

"Who just called out to me in that clingy voice, saying, 'Boss, come on'? You'll see the consequence in your next salary!" That was a joke I often made back in December 2005, and it suddenly comes to mind. It was a time of mounting deficits and an uncertain future.

I think this is my limit. It's really tough. Perhaps the most challenging time in my life. But I can smile because it's also the happiest time. Recalling those difficult yet joyful times, thinking of today, and envisioning the future, I reassure myself, *Sujin Lee, you are surrounded by people who truly care about you, and you are doing fine.*

My loved ones, because of you, I find strength even on days when my mind is troubled. Thank you, Seon-hwa, for enduring tough times and being a steadfast supporter. I always feel apologetic to you, and regret not having done more and better.

No matter where you go, if you maintain the smile that you had when you first joined the company, you'll be a tremendous asset. Team leader Yoo, who joined us during challenging times and has contributed immensely to the company, I fondly remember the days of sharing ramen for lunch and am grateful for your presence. Even though you can be an 'ice queen' sometimes, I appreciate your unwavering dedication to your duties.

Koo Bon-gil, you monster! In my heart, Team Leader Koo Bon-gil is forever a monster, embodying fiercely burning passion. I feared his passion might diminish too soon, but it has continued burning like an unquenchable fire. Hence, I always smile whenever I see him.

Jong-gyu, whom I got to know through my friend Jae-kyung, is truly dedicated to development and always maintains a positive attitude. His reassuring presence and willingness to handle anything make him a valuable confidante. I've had a jinx with those of blood type AB, but Jong-gyu helped break that. Let's continue to foster such good relationships moving forward.

Jae-won initially left a less favourable impression – I couldn't quite gauge what he brought to the table, so I twice met with him for meals to interview him. Eventually, I was captivated by his intense passion and genuine caring attitude toward Yanolja. Contrary to my initial impression, it's wonderful to know such a gentle and caring soul. I look forward to seeing him lead Yanolja brilliantly alongside Team Leader Bon-gil, his friendly rival and partner.

Chan-jin, the grumpy yet mischievous one, has pleasantly surprised me. It's rewarding to see him becoming more accustomed to work routines, developing an interest in his job, and enhancing his skills. I am thankful to Chan-jin, who, despite seeming grumpy, is committed to his role and always considerate of others.

Myeong-sun, who is always quiet, almost as if she's not there, manages to handle work accurately and delicately on the spot. I always feel reassured when I entrust tasks to Myeong-sun; I know she'll complete them right and well. Also known as Ye-rim, I hope you remain a cherished person with an unchanging heart like you are now.

So-hyun, with whom I feel most at ease. She left a lasting impression on me with her chewing gum and phone during the job interview. Was I more nervous than her? I appreciate her positive mindset and the comfort she brings, like a friend from my hometown.

Hee-jeong, who is only quiet around me. A woman who knows design and is therefore a valuable member of our team. Despite initial hesitations due to our work's lack of organization and consistency, I am grateful she chose to join us and become an asset to Yanolja. Hee-jeong, you're even more beautiful when you smile, so I hope to see more of your smiles.

August 30, 2007, 01:03

I SHALL START WITH
FOLLOWING THE RIGHT TRACK
INSTEAD OF THE EASY AND FAST TRACK

When you harbour malicious intentions in order to move quickly, tell lies for an easier path, or deceive yourself with excuses, it seems the heart eventually returns the misdeeds to you like an arrow. What exactly is the 'right track'? "Do I truly have a 'right track' in my heart?" There are times when my mind becomes clouded and impatient, and I find myself raising my voice. It's not easy to adhere to standards and navigate a way forward while firmly holding the rudder.

Time gradually runs out and the day of reckoning approaches, but things still appear disorganized. Sometimes, I fear this chaos could become a loophole, presenting a golden opportunity for someone else. When I physically and mentally relax, curb my desires, and follow the right path, I'll find lasting comfort.

Managing a small company initially seemed easy, but over time, it has become a heavier burden on my mind and increasingly challenging. It feels like a series of trials, akin to the growing pains of a child. However, I am confident that the company will continue to grow. Even if there's a brief period of stagnation, it doesn't equate to a full stop. If there's a path I'm committed to in my mind, and if I stay conscious of it, I believe that someday I'll achieve what I aim for.

December 20, 2007, 19:47

THOSE PROBLEMS ARE WHAT I LIVE FOR

When running a company, encountering problems is inevitable, just as it is in life. Isn't living itself about facing challenges and seeking solutions? Since my youth, I've encountered many issues, and as the president of a company, I grapple with even more needing immediate attention or strategic direction for the future.

Being in a decision-making position, I'm constantly weighing the pros and cons in my head, deciding on solutions, and occasionally accepting the need to let go. The role of a CEO demands continual analysis and judgment, exposing and refining one's decision-making abilities. However, my decisions and solutions are not always correct; sometimes they lead to mistakes or even failures.

When the company was smaller, our direction often seemed unclear until I addressed the immediate problems. I had to find solutions one way or another, so most issues were resolved quickly and easily. While some were complex, most could be tackled with commitment. At the time, even the less-challenging problems felt burdensome, requiring my utmost effort. Yet, in hindsight, they were solvable with a bit of effort, and each resolved problem enabled us to level up.

The problem with a growing company is the simultaneous emergence of multiple issues. These include challenges related to people, technology, funding, market changes, rapid technological advancements and political factors, among others. Some are long-term challenges, while others demand immediate solutions, testing the company's capabilities. When considering solutions, there are various criteria to ponder. However,

I tend to focus on one key question: how will it affect our future value?

Opting for immediate advantages might make things easier now, but it can create a vicious cycle leading to larger problems in the future. The decision to forego a seemingly advantageous solution in the present is a challenge not easily overcome. Individuals might naturally seek to maximize their current favourable circumstances; however, a company is not just one person's possession.

I believe that a company should prioritize the future value it brings to its employees over immediate gains. Its true power is realized only when it exists in harmony with its workforce. Of course, during tough times, a company's immediate survival takes precedence: if a company cannot survive, there is no future for its employees. Only after a survival strategy is in place can we ensure a future. And focusing on the future serves as evidence that prioritizing survival is a strategic choice.

Some suggest that the solution to a problem should be future-oriented, but putting this into practice is easier said than done. If it were so straightforward, everyone would excel in identifying and resolving issues. When confronted with a problem, people often find themselves either blank-minded or trapped in one-sided thinking. They ask, "Why has this misfortune befallen me? Is this a situation beyond my control?" Rather than tackling the issue head-on, many resort to making excuses, such as "This isn't my fault; it was caused by someone else."

This reaction is, in a way, natural. How resilient can humans be? As a child, you might have started crying upon seeing a drop of blood, even if it wasn't painful. Or consider how a tiny thorn in your finger, though not life-threatening, can cause significant annoyance and discomfort. Perhaps being a leader is a divine task, endlessly testing human willpower. As a boss, you must decipher and contemplate the nature of problems amid countless challenges. Failure to do so will inevitably lead to consequences for your business direction, compelling you to try and stay afloat.

I once faced an online service disruption while running a business. This issue quickly expanded to encompass web page and mobile app development, member trends and needs, and even trends among business partners. As the problem's impact grew, it began to affect internal communication among my employees. Eventually, it escalated into a tangible issue that put pressure on me to swiftly find a solution. Solving one problem didn't mean the end of our challenges; as soon as one was resolved, others began to emerge. With time, I've come to understand that a multitude of problems doesn't necessarily signify something wrong. Instead, it can indicate that the company is functioning well and holds future value.

If you stay at home doing nothing, the only problem you face is figuring out your next meal. However, the moment you take action to earn a living, you're met with a myriad of challenges. Sometimes we solve these problems easily and, once resolved, they become part of our daily life and culture. However, even solved problems can evolve over time, leading to new challenges. Before getting married, I thought marriage would solve all my problems. But post-marriage, a whole new set of issues emerged, like dealing with in-laws, parenting and housing. These too became matters that needed addressing.

The presence of many problems indicates that you are progressing by solving them, and encountering more challenges as you advance. However, you cannot simply sit back and let life pass you by just because you dislike problems. It's only by actively engaging with and enjoying the process of problem-solving that we develop self-belief, independence, a sense of accomplishment and the courage to make life more meaningful.

We are always faced with multiple problems. Growth occurs when we examine these problems closely to identify potential future value, and then act, rather than attempting to avoid them. I often wonder how many problems I need to address, present and solve, whether as president or otherwise. My hope is that problems will not be seen as something to fear, but as opportunities that bring purpose and joy. In the end, I hope to always remember that these problems are what I truly live for.

NOT EVERYONE CAN SUCCEED

Isn't success something everyone aspires to? Reflecting on my 20s, I often found myself thinking, "I hope I become successful." That desire for success was ever-present in my thoughts. Perhaps that's why, today, I find myself in a position where I can think more wisely and envision the future more clearly than in my younger years. In that sense, I consider my younger days to have been successful.

While everyone dreams of success, not everyone achieves it. Why is that? Yesterday, an employee came to me with a personal issue. He had planned a meeting between his and his fiancée's parents to discuss their upcoming marriage. However, just a day before the meeting, his girlfriend called off the engagement. He was heartbroken. In his story, I saw a reflection of my own younger self, when I, too, had little to my name.

I vividly recalled the days when I grappled with harsh realities, and I deeply empathized with him. As a listener, all I could offer was sympathy, but he was the one facing the issue. What was his next step? Perhaps he needed to transform himself into a man of confidence. He wasn't unrealistic, nor did he have personality flaws, and he certainly wasn't insincere. But if he was being misjudged based on his financial status, wouldn't he need to become someone who could prove his reliability and trustworthiness to others?

So, how can individuals who start with nothing, like I did, build confidence and achieve success? Some expect to find success tomorrow by working hard today, but it's not always that straightforward.

In hindsight, I realize that my past experiences have collectively shaped who I am today. The real challenge is in the countless battles you have with yourself every day. Overcoming oneself is no easy feat. It's simple to advise others with phrases like "Don't do that" or "You're wrong," but it's much harder to say to yourself, "No, don't do it" or "You are wrong." For us ordinary people, it's difficult to exercise self-restraint and control our actions. However, when we do manage to achieve this self-control, it appears that we can ultimately win the battle against ourselves.

Immediate success is a rarity anywhere in the world. Success requires preparation. Top students don't achieve good grades effortlessly. Top athletes weren't simply born with their abilities. They dedicated considerable effort to reach their current levels. Success follows a similar path. If you constantly resolve to succeed, saying, "I will succeed. I definitely will," but your daily actions contradict this goal, or if your efforts are no different than anyone else's, what do you think your chances of success are?

I wanted to share with that employee the mindset I held when I was young. Live each day confidently, hold your head high. Today may not conjure up miracles for tomorrow, but if you live each day with even a 5% change, these small changes will accumulate over one, five and ten years. At least 5% of a year, or 5% of a decade, will likely be filled with successful moments. If you live and work diligently for 50% of the time with a transformed mindset, 50% of those ten years will be times of success. And with such dedication, I am confident that by then you will have already become a successful person.

There seem to be several conditions for success, with the first being 'continuous thinking.' This means constantly contemplating success to the point of self-brainwashing. You must master your thoughts so that your actions naturally align with them. When something is consciously thought about continuously, it eventually permeates even the subconscious.

I remember a lesson from my youth, from a teacher, on how to become an assemblyman representing a rural town. The advice was simple: greet people every time you see them and pick up trash whenever you encounter it. Do this for ten or 20 years, and you will be recognized as a "man with a bright personality" and a "dedicated individual" in your community. Initially, these actions might feel pretentious, but with consistency, they become habitual and ingrained, turning into a natural part of your behaviour. Life reaches a point where not doing these actions feels unnatural.

At first, this practice is difficult, but over time, people begin to recognize you. They greet you before you can say hello and emulate your actions by not littering. The teacher explained that such virtuous actions eventually return to you as rewards. As a young person, I didn't fully grasp the moral of this lesson. But now, as I stand on my own in the world, bearing my responsibilities and duties, those words continually inspire me. New shoes may feel foreign and uncomfortable at first, but after wearing them for a while, they mould to your feet and become comfortable. Such is the way of the world.

The second condition for success is mindset. It seems that success is elusive if you make enemies. You must strive to be someone who acts morally and gets along with others. This approach ensures you are surrounded by good people who will support you in times of trouble or opportunity. No matter how strong your belief in success, if your intentions are malevolent, people will not stand by you. It's said that everything in the world is accomplished through people, so how can one succeed without the support of others? Regardless of how skilled or capable you are, I believe that success achieved without harmony is lonely and unsustainable.

There are three types of leaders: brave generals, wise generals and virtuous generals. Among them, the most important is said to be the virtuous general. I would like to add another category: the people-friendly leader. As we live in a community of brave, wise and virtuous people, I aspire to be a leader who has those people standing by me. When you act well and in accordance with your heart, it becomes easier for your influence to spread, and you can achieve more together. You are better recognized because you have people who will collabourate, share joy and even extend that joy further. Ultimately, people become the cornerstone that creates the conditions for success.

The third key to success is will – the determination to make something happen. Regardless of the situation, you need to be determined and believe that you can succeed. Even if you aspire to succeed and are a considerate individual, how can you act without the will to persevere and overcome crises and slumps? Success often sprouts from working harder than others. However, the younger generation today seems to feel overwhelmed by the notion of striving "more than others." They might wonder how it's possible to excel when everyone else appears to be fiercely competitive. Yet, it's crucial to assess reality objectively. Are you truly making each day count, or are you just finding excuses for a lack of will? The resolve to act today, not tomorrow, lays the groundwork for life-altering changes a decade down the line. This is something I can assert with confidence, based on my own experiences.

The fourth factor is a proper understanding of money. The perception of money is extremely important. While the pursuit of success should not be solely about money, it is often a means to an end. In contemporary society, whether one is an athlete, entrepreneur, freelancer, artist or broadcaster, the amount of money earned frequently denotes one's status and level of success. It's essential to grasp why the magnitude of financial resources matters. Money should not be the ultimate goal – that leads to enslavement by wealth. Instead, understanding its role and managing it wisely is key to genuine success.

However, it's essential to recognize the metrics for growth, and let's be clear: a practical measure is the amount of money you receive. Additionally, the more money you have, the broader the range of actions you can undertake. The key point isn't merely having a lot of money; rather, it's understanding that substantial financial resources expand the scope of what you can achieve. Money should be seen as a means to enhance life and enable you to pursue your desires. If acquiring wealth is your sole goal, earning money will always be a challenge. However, if you approach it from the perspective of "How much money allows me to do what I want?" you will learn to use money effectively and open up more opportunities. How you spend money is just as crucial as how you earn it. I believe that success achieved without a proper understanding of money is mere pretense.

Ultimately, success is not handed to you by others; it's something you think about, act upon and create for yourself. No one else can achieve it for you. If you delay doing something that only you can do, if you fail to contemplate and act upon it, then success will never be within your grasp.

2008

FOURTH YEAR SINCE FOUNDING

SET SPECIFIC GOALS AND STRIVE TO ACHIEVE THEM

The arrival of a new year often prompts us to make resolutions. At the start, there's a sense of having ample time to work toward our goals. However, a look back at the previous year's sales quickly reveals the urgency; time is indeed limited. The regret from 2007 lingers – if only I could have increased sales by $2,000 per month, we would have met our target sales.

Goals, target sales, incentives – we exist on the testing ground of reality, judged by various standards. Recognition comes only with achievement. This reminds me of school vacations when homework was assigned. Spending the entire break playing and then scrambling to complete homework at the last minute led to anxiety and a heavy heart. Sometimes, the burden feels so overwhelming that you might even give up on the homework entirely. In contrast, completing homework early allows you to enjoy the rest of the vacation without the nagging weight of unfinished tasks.

This year, my aim is to achieve sales of $2 million, more than doubling last year's figure. The initial target is set at $1.6 million, but let's set our sights higher. To reach $2 million, I need to analyse sales meticulously and devise a strategy. Simply dividing $2 million over 12 months seems daunting. My hope is to make this a year where we can achieve $2 million in 11 months, allowing us a month of carefree rest.

To achieve the annual sales goal of $2 million, I need to secure $1,800 in sales each month. This translates to $540 thousand per quarter. It's crucial to quickly figure out how to reach $540 thousand every quarter and to establish a detailed plan. I must ensure our goals transcend mere wishes and aspirations. Only by doing this can my next goals become more robust and definite.

It was disappointing not to meet our sales goal in 2007, but we must learn from this and avoid ending 2008 with the same regrets. Our objectives for 2008 include achieving $2 million in sales and reaching a membership of 500,000. To attain 500,000 members, an additional 410,000 people need to join. This means that, for the remaining 359 days of the year, an average of 1,142 people must sign up daily. I need to devise a strategy to make this possible.

The number of potential members who haven't joined yet represents a challenge I must confront continuously. To hit the $2 million target, I must generate $180 thousand in sales monthly and $6,000 daily. Failing to find a way to increase daily sales to $6,000 would turn my goal into an unfulfiled dream.

Setting a goal is a serious commitment. Once made, it's my responsibility to find ways to honour it. Adhering to this principle is fundamental to achieving success.

January 7, 2008, 01:04

KEEP THE SAME COMMITMENT AND DEVOTION AS IN THE BEGINNING

The number ten cannot exist without the number one. The company, which started in deficit, has been gradually taking shape and building up over the past three years. Just as you need to accumulate ones to make ten, I hope that the efforts of my past days will contribute to future growth. Initiating something with determination means I've completed the most crucial step toward success. To ensure comprehensive success, I must continue moving forward with the same commitment and devotion I had at the beginning of this journey.

February 12, 2008, 08:51

I MUST KEEP PUSHING FORWARD WITH WHAT I ENVISIONED IN THE BEGINNING

You may start a business with great ideas and intentions, but if they don't persist, you'll just be left with regrets and complacency in the future. I must not forget the principle of pushing forward what I have started until the end. Knowing that consistent thinking and effort will eventually bring my vision to life, I am committed to creating situations where I can take the necessary actions, starting with the small ones.

February 14, 2008, 11:40

ASPIRING TO ACHIEVE THE DREAMS
I IMAGINE ABOVE THE CLOUDS

There are times when I momentarily escape reality and find myself floating above the clouds. The visions I entertain there represent aspirations yet to be realized. This is what makes it so exciting. Sometimes, it's challenging and taxing to bring these unmaterialized dreams to life. But I am aware that perseverance can turn imagination into reality. That's the reason I continue to push forward every day.

My life has always been characterized more by complexity and speed than by leisure and relaxation. Perhaps I've grown accustomed to it, maybe even relish it. Will I become a perpetual dreamer among the clouds? Will I ever truly have the chance to lie down and rest in their embrace? I understand that this depends entirely on me and no one else. That's the reason I keep pressing forward, as I always have.

March 25, 2008

THINKING AND OBSERVING: THE HALLMARKS OF TRULY WEALTHY INDIVIDUALS

What lies at the core of my strengths? Perhaps it is the ability to think and imagine. Reflecting on what has brought me to my current position, I realize that the driving force behind my growth has been thinking, which originated from my aspirations for the future. This highlights the importance of thought, as it is the critical starting point for self-transformation. No one else can change me. However, don't we often alter our actions and words based on our own determination and aspirations? Therefore, thoughts become the power source that drives me and the standard by which I act.

Long before I started my business, I was full of imagination. When I was struggling financially, I imagined being wealthy. During my college years, I dreamt of receiving a scholarship because I needed it. In school, I envisioned receiving a special military service exemption, as I needed to earn money rather than enlisting. This imagination led to tangible results. As a teenager, I acquired skills to earn money quickly. After studying technology in high school, I went on to a university in that field. Already possessing the skills, I adapted faster than my peers and earned a scholarship. My technical proficiency and academic performance landed me a highly sought-after job in the defense industry, allowing me to earn while fulfiling my military service. While working in defense, I acknowledged my limitations as an employee. I never ceased imagining. I constantly thought about ways to earn well, shaping the trajectory of my journey.

After completing my military service, I focused on stock investment and auctions. Soon, I found myself needing to save some seed money, leading me to take a job as a cleaner at a motel that offered room, board, and a decent salary. It was physically demanding, but it enabled me to earn. However, working 365 days a year without personal time restricted my life and prevented me from enjoying my youth. This led me to seek a system that would allow me to earn money without physical labour. Today's Yanolja was born out of this quest. I envisioned a scenario where I could earn by using my intellect, with money being deposited into my account even when I wasn't physically at work. The concept in the book *Rich Dad, Poor Dad,* which I read in my early 20s, resonated with me. The author stated that true wealth is achieved by creating a structure that allows money to continuously flow into your account without working. Ultimately, what a truly wealthy person must do is think and observe. This means that work should be done with the mind, not just the body.

To me, thinking is a uniquely fascinating activity. Some people dislike engaging in deep thought, often postponing it or claiming they don't give it much consideration. However, consistently avoiding thought can become a habit, transforming potentially favourable situations into unfavourable ones, and even turning your life upside down. That's why thinking is so important. The more one thinks, the more varied our perspectives become. When problems arise, a thinking person can respond quickly. Naturally, someone who has engaged in a lot of thinking tends to have an advantage in most situations.

I'm not particularly smart. Even if I were, my academic background is quite modest compared to many startup founders. When you observe today's startup founders, you'll notice they often boast impressive educational credentials. I envy them, but I don't envy their academic achievements. I am captivated by the brilliance of their minds. In conversations with them, I am fascinated by their thought processes and find their intellectual agility marvellous. I envy them for being able to engage in their work with a depth of imagination and thoughtfulness that surpasses mine, as someone who has primarily learned through field experience.

Nowadays, there are many books that explain the importance of imagination and how to cultivate it. Young people are already well-informed on this subject. So, when discussing imagination, they might respond, "I know. Everybody knows that." Perhaps they're right. Maybe everyone does know. However, what I want to emphasize is that ultimately, it all comes down to taking action. Possessing great knowledge is one thing, but acting on it is an entirely different matter.

Abundant imagination and extensive thinking are crucial keys to transforming reality. They represent the initial step that ultimately shapes your life and is the only way to truly change yourself. This is a lesson I learned through my own experiences while running a business. However, these days, many young startup founders seem to understand this right from the start. As they are already ahead in this regard, I find myself needing to imagine and discover more ways to survive and grow in this competitive world. In society, and similarly in the business realm, competing with those who are more educated is inevitable. I constantly ponder how to overcome my limited knowledge and succeed in such competitions.

My routine involves repeatedly envisioning a future where I excel in what I do best, organizing my thoughts about the current reality and integrating lessons from past experiences. Every day, my mind engages in a battle with these thoughts. If I stop thinking, how would the value of my existence change? My position as the leader of Yanolja would vanish, dealing a significant blow to the rest of my life. My strength lies in my ability to imagine possibilities for Yanolja. I may not be adept at envisioning general social life or other companies, but it's a great blessing to be engaged in what I excel at. Additionally, the ability to earn a living and lead a life while doing what I am best at is immensely valuable.

I recall a TV commercial that proclaimed, "Expect something beyond your imagination." To me, that encapsulates reality. If you diligently engage in imagination and thought, one day it will manifest into reality, and you can become the protagonist of that reality. Employment and economic challenges are daunting, often leading to feelings of self-doubt. Our life story often seems to be about navigating hardships, but time inevitably moves forward. If you harbour pessimistic thoughts, as time passes, life becomes more challenging. Conversely, if you think clearly and positively about the path you wish to take, you will likely make at least one step forward in your journey.

As someone who has long held onto imagination through tough times and seen those dreams become reality, I assert this boldly: cultivate the habit of imagining and thinking. The more challenging life is, the greater the need to overcome these difficulties by envisioning a brighter future and engaging in more useful thoughts. We live in an era where imagination can be transformed into reality. While this transformation doesn't occur overnight, if you persistently focus on the same vision for one, five or ten years, it will inevitably materialize. Trust in this process, as it is a proven formula. Ultimately, the inception of a future better than the present starts with the power of imagining and thinking.

LET'S NOT JUDGE THE WORLD BY LOOKING AT IT THROUGH A SMALL WINDOW

Suddenly, I find myself wondering what I am doing. Am I living my life viewing the world through a small window, mistakenly believing that this limited view is all there is? What does the world mean to me? What is my place in it? How does my perception of the world differ from how the world perceives me? It's time to reconsider whether I have forgotten how to see the world correctly, amid the trivialities that often occupy my thoughts.

April 28, 2008

CALCULATING MY LIFE BY COUNTING BACKWARDS FROM 2058

I ponder whether I am so absorbed in the present, or naively believing that this moment will last forever, that I neglect the future. Or perhaps I am living contentedly in the present without much thought for what lies ahead.

In 2058, I will be 81 years old. I might be counting down my days or, perhaps, I might no longer be alive. When I reflect in 2058, I hope to say, "Yes, my life was truly worthwhile. I can rest in peace, knowing I have no regrets." I hope not to end my days thinking, "It was a life full of troubles. If given another chance, I would live differently." It's hard to envision, but someday, I'll become an old man, just as our ancestors did. However, when I ask myself, "What am I preparing for?" I realize that I'm not just thinking about what will happen in 2009, 2015 or 2020.

No, I'm not properly preparing for the future. Such neglect is foolish. In 2017, I will turn 40 years old. Middle age, which once seemed so distant, is approaching faster than I anticipated. By 2030, I will be 53 years old. Although no one relishes the idea of aging, I should ensure stability at that age, rather than grappling with challenges like many others. If I spend my youth without considering these aspects, I'm certain I'll look back with regret, wishing to turn back time to my younger years. In this reality, what does a good life mean? What should be the driving force that motivates me to focus more on the future, rather than dwelling on the past?

The actions I take now will accumulate and shape what I can do at that age. It's time to seriously consider where to focus my thoughts, actions and heart. The year 2058 is not as distant as it seems.

June 23, 2008

LIMITS BECOME STEPPING-STONES ONCE THEY ARE OVERCOME

On days when my mind is clear, the future seems vivid and distinct. I don't feel the usual fear and anxiety that intermittently plague me. Being a young man shouldering heavy burdens isn't easy. Tasks I expected to accomplish with ease grow in weight and complexity. Despite my desire to run straight and light, I find myself facing obstacles in all directions. A seasoned driver might effortlessly navigate these, but I am not one yet. I'm constantly aware of my limits, grappling with lingering anxiety and fear. However, I must remember a truth I've always believed: limits become stepping-stones once they are overcome.

Humans often wrestle with thoughts about the distant and near future, the present and the past. Perhaps my anxiety and troubles would lessen if I fully embraced the truth that my past self has shaped who I am today, and my present self is shaping who I will be in the future. Dwelling on idiotic ideas and thoughts that only fuel my fears and delusions is unproductive. Instead, I should focus on disciplining myself to be free from these futile notions.

To me, a mentor is found in the truths I discover in books. To find and practice these truths, I must think, for the future lies within those thoughts. My actions and thoughts today are what determine the value of my existence in the future. Therefore, I will think, especially on days like this when my mind is exceptionally clear. I will envision a hopeful image of myself in the future and the success that will follow. Deep thought is crucial.

August 28, 2008

$300 MILLION IS NOT ENOUGH, AND LIFE IS BORING

How did I manage to keep moving forward during the days when reality was bleak and the path ahead was obscured? It's clear that my driving force was an obsession with and hopes for the future. That was true in my past. But what about now? Do I have a clear vision of the future I dream about? Is it constantly in my thoughts? Is my heart still fuelled by passion?

A future that flickers in your mind but fails to stir your heart is nothing more than a mirage. Am I advancing toward the future without real confidence?

Once again, I turn to a book for inspiration, seeking assurance in an uncertain future. I realize that simply reassuring myself with thoughts like, "It will be okay," "Let's work hard," or "Let's try" isn't enough to dispel the uncertainties.

I need to set detailed, tangible goals and focus solely on achieving them. There's only one month left in 2008, and when the new year arrives, I will inevitably set new goals. However, the goals that reside in my mind and heart should be unwavering, constant until the day I die or, more precisely, until they are firmly imprinted in my heart.

It's time to reevaluate what truly matters. Aiming for $300 billion is not sufficient. Life is boring.

December 1, 2008

2009
FIFTH YEAR SINCE FOUNDING

EVERYONE HAS A STARTING POINT IN LIFE

Every life journey begins with a starting point. At the start, we encounter both excitement and fear. But inevitably, we tend to lean toward one of these emotions. The key to achieving success lies in embracing the excitement rather than succumbing to the fear.

"What brought me here?"

This question alone is profound. I've reached this point driven by the vision of success in my mind, not because I had ample money or exceptional intellect. Initiating something new is daunting, but I hope this apprehension won't hinder me. Instead, I want it to be an integral part of my life's journey, guiding me toward success. I firmly believe this is achievable. Different ways of thinking can alter the future. I aim to run forward with such intensity that my heart feels like it's about to burst. Then, I'll take a moment to look back. Perhaps that's my responsibility. At this new starting line, I hope to remain fully engaged in the present, rather than dwelling on what I've done in the past or what I'll do in the future.

January 4, 2009

IF A TOWER BUILT WITH GREAT EFFORT COLLAPSES, I'LL REBUILD IT

Crisis strikes in an instant. I've just completed inspecting rooms at Ellie Hotel, a lodging business I operated to launch franchise branding. This experience reaffirmed my need for dedicated inspection staff. The state of the rooms was the poorest I've encountered. It's astonishing how quickly conditions deteriorated. I acknowledge this as my failing. I should have been more vigilant, rather than neglecting management with the complacent belief that everything would consistently be at its best.

Confronted with the frustration of seeing a tower, built with painstaking effort, collapse, I ended up venting loudly in front of my employees. Perhaps that's why I'm feeling deeply unsettled. Yet, I remain confident. Today, we may not be perfect, but I am sure we will soon stand up and run forward again. I hope, and believe, that our employees share this sentiment.

We harbour a dream. We also possess the strength to rebuild what has been lost. With this strength, we are destined for success. Life would be much easier if everything unfolded as planned. But reality often proves more challenging, requiring us to build our dreams sincerely, one step at a time. That is the essence of life.

January 6, 2009, 20:18

CONCEITED PASSION LEADS TO FOOLISH ACTIONS

Sometimes, I wonder if my past success in overcoming hardships has led me to underestimate the difficulties in the world. I must remember that such arrogance could prove to be my downfall. The economy is increasingly challenging, and the future of our company is not guaranteed to be smooth. Our current growth is not guaranteed to last forever.

Just because everything is fine now doesn't mean it will remain so in the future. It's a time for careful consideration and reevaluation of our strategies and goals. Even Yanolja is not immune to the looming shadow of recession. What approach should we take in such times? We possess a valuable and potent weapon: passion. However, overconfidence in our passion can lead to amateurish and clumsy actions, with painful consequences.

The size of our website is expanding, but this has not translated into increased sales. Revenue from top banner advertisements, a major source of our income, has significantly dropped compared to the end of last year. Similarly, earnings from membership is declining. Yet, we haven't developed a new profit model. Sustaining current sales is crucial for buying time to explore new revenue streams, but it's uncertain how long we can maintain existing sales amid this economic slump.

If I can't generate new profits within the next few months to a year, our future is in jeopardy. How can I create new revenue streams? Developing a completely new model is challenging. Our focus should be on maximizing our existing resources. This could involve expanding our network of affiliated stores, increasing membership or linking dating course services to sales. I'm not sure what the right solution is, but I keep thinking endlessly. I hope to gain the clarity to look in the right direction.

March 4, 2009

DOING MY BEST IS MY FATE AND LIFE

I feel something within my grasp. I'm not certain what it is, but I sense that I'm on the verge of seizing it. No one can predict the future, but I believe that it is merely the result of the present I am shaping. Whether by chance or necessity, it is a consequence of the now. To attain something, you must think hard about it and act accordingly. The future becomes bleak if you surrender halfway, fearing failure and denying possibilities.

Maintain a positive outlook. Always smile and do your utmost. That is both fate and life. Such opportunities, luck and realities don't come to everyone, but they have come to me. I won't let them slip away. I will believe in myself and my future, confident that it will lead to success.

March 5, 2009

I NEED A DETERMINATION
NEVER TO GIVE UP

My weight was consistently 150 lbs from 1996 to 2003, during and shortly after my college years. However, it increased to 160 lbs in 2005, and by the end of that year, it was 190 lbs. Finally, it has returned to its normal range.

When was the last time I weighed 157 lbs? I started dieting on March 10 at 180 lbs, and now, 70 days later, I am at 157 lbs. Despite occasionally succumbing to overeating, I quickly regained my senses and didn't give up. It worked. I once thought losing weight was impossible, but I succeeded in just 70 days. This experience illustrates human vulnerability. All it took was a firm resolve and consistent effort, but how often did I lose that determination, thinking it was too hard? How many times did I fail to lose weight? Humans may be weak creatures, but with a singular focus, our chances of success can dramatically increase.

THE FUTURE IS YOURS AS LONG AS YOU ARE DETERMINED NOT TO GIVE UP

There may be struggles and moments when you need to pause, but with your soul and mind fully invested, and through your actions, the future is yours to claim. The journey to the future starts by questioning how you want to live. If you perceive your dreams as distant fantasies or akin to winning the lottery, transforming them into reality becomes challenging.

Change only starts to manifest when you think persistently about your goals and gradually bring them to life through action. I was once a poor sales staff member and business owner, dependent on rides because I couldn't afford my own car. But that's not who I am today. I once viewed motel owners as people from a different, unreachable world. Now, I am one of those people. I used to be 180 lbs with a belly overhanging my belt, but today, I am trying to build six-pack abs.

When asked about my dream, I used to say, "I want to make $30,000 in sales each month and not worry about paying my employees." Now, my answer has evolved to, "My dream is $300 million. Yanolja World." Gradually, I'm starting to believe that this dream could expand into the globalization of Yanolja World, reaching $3 billion.

My life is not subject to change brought about by others; it transforms based on my current thoughts. I cast a spell on myself. I persist without giving up, continually taking action. If I press on energetically and need to rest, I'll slow down, but I'll never stop. Doing so, I believe that one day

I'll encounter the biggest, proudest and most confident version of myself. A life where you see yourself as confident, irrespective of failure or success, is a truly successful life.

May 21, 2009

SOMETIMES YOU JUST HAVE TO BE PATIENT AND PERSISTENT

May has swiftly passed, and June, marking the end of the first half of the year, has begun. The remaining task for 2009 seems to be preparing for the future. Now, as the Yanolja brand transitions from its introduction phase to the early stages of growth, we must find ways to provide robust support to ensure its longevity. Many companies are like candles flickering precariously in the wind, with the burden often falling heavily on employees and stakeholders.

True success stories start when you can sustain efforts over a long period. For this, seed money is essential – in business terms, it means capital. We have secured some, but it's not enough for significant moves. At the very least, I should possess enough resources to achieve goals without risking everything.

Overextending and committing 100% of the company's resources to a single venture is a risky move. I've learned this from experience. If I lose my pace and try to match others' speed, I risk collapsing before reaching the finish line. True success comes with patience and the ability to endure short-term setbacks.

I will view 2009 as a year of patience, a time to prepare for tasting success. I aim to secure as much cash flow as possible to lay the groundwork for reviving another strong brand in 2010.

May 31, 2009

GREED LEADS TO FAILURE

It's important to ask ourselves, "What will truly enrich me?" We need to understand correctly how greed can lead to failure. Let's seriously contemplate what is necessary for success. We shouldn't pursue minor profits at the cost of earning criticism. It's better to clear our minds and choose the right path.

Let's consider the concept of coexistence. We should think about what we can offer and what we will gain in return. If there is someone to whom I am willing to give what I have, that person can be a valuable ally on the path to success. Now, it's time to revisit my initial determination and reflect on what actions I should take and what plans I should make. It's time to return to the mindset I had when I started from nothing, seeking ways to support everyone. Fulfilment and joy that serve only me are merely fleeting forms of greed, leaving long-lasting regrets.

Admittedly, relinquishing greed is not easy, but I can start slowly, beginning with small steps. I am committed to building Yanolja as a compassionate company that benefits everyone involved. I must never forget that this approach is the key to Yanolja's prosperity.

June 15, 2009, 23:29

I AM THANKFUL ON THE LAST
PAYDAY OF 2009

Today marks the last payday of the year. The year has passed swiftly, yet it also feels long and profound. Looking back on 2009, it seems to have sped by without major surprises, but it certainly wasn't an easy journey. In many ways, it may have been the most significant year yet. I don't often pause to consider what motivates me; I simply follow my drive and give my all.

There are times when I feel lazy, but these moments are just brief pauses. I've never lost sight of my direction. I sincerely hope that 2009 will be remembered as a year I'd like to revisit when reflecting on the most beautiful days of my life. Now, it seems, is the time to prepare for another year. Back in 2005, paydays were a source of anxiety, but I'm grateful for how much the company has grown since then. I'll remember those nerve-wracking days, be thankful for today, and continue to fuel my passion. That's how I believe I should express my gratitude.

December 11, 2009, 00:11

IT'S A NERVE-WRACKING SITUATION, BUT LET'S NOT BECOME TIMID

Hotel O has finally opened. Yet I'm reminded again that embarking on new challenges is never easy. No matter the endeavour, there's always a problem to solve, and as soon as one is resolved, another emerges. The sense of weariness is particularly acute on days that feel like the endless process of peeling an onion, layer by layer. However, this weariness cannot be a reason to stand still. I am aware that now is the time for real commitment. The situation is fraught with reasons for nervousness, but I must not become timid. This is what is expected of me, these are the challenges I must face. There hasn't been a problem yet that couldn't be solved. These challenges must be addressed and overcome by any means necessary, so all I can do is embrace another challenge and invest my whole heart and soul into it.

The project isn't perfect, and there seems to be many flaws. But this is a part of my life that I must embrace. What I need to do is to accept it as my life and give it my best effort. I don't need anything else. It may appear modest at first, but I am filled with confidence. Even if there's doubt, I choose to believe in my confidence. I am convinced that if I don't give up until the end, I will transcend my limits and turn them into steppingstones toward further growth.

December 21, 2009, 03:38

* I chose to eschew conventional methods, opting instead to remodel the hotel with new interior finishing materials before opening. The process had its challenges; the interior didn't turn out as expected and numerous flaws were identified. Ultimately, though, we managed to rectify all the issues and even added unique features to the interior, much to the satisfaction of our customers.

EVERY DAY IS A WAR THAT
YOU CANNOT RETREAT FROM

It feels as though every day is a battle. As time progresses, the weight of being the president of a company grows heavier. The burden increases as the company expands. This is a natural progression, yet there are moments when I yearn for a day's respite. However, the relentless demands of daily tasks mean that the company's work has become an integral part of my identity, and my life has become synonymous with the company. This is my destiny, the result of my own making. Perhaps I can alleviate stress by learning to enjoy this relentless battle more in the days ahead.

Since this is just the beginning, I should strive to find enjoyment. Being able to derive pleasure from such challenges is a skill. This won't conclude in a day or two; everything has a beginning, a course that it follows and an outcome. And from each outcome stems another new beginning. Whether I like it or not, this cycle has already begun and will continue. Therefore, I shouldn't allow myself to be overwhelmed by fear or heaviness. Accepting challenges that evoke strong feelings can lead to an uncontrollable slump.

Living as a boss is increasingly proving to be far from the ideal daily life I had envisioned. However, if this is the path I must follow, shouldn't I embrace it wholeheartedly? I need to be more patient, broaden my thinking and act with a combination of strength and flexibility. And most importantly, I must never lose sight of my goal. The moment I lose it, I risk falling. I must not give up simply because the task is challenging. Regardless of what others say or how much I am shaken, I can stubbornly pursue my goal. That steadfastness will lead to success. If I am to face an unending war, I will have to push my limits and devise a clear strategy and tactics to succeed.

December 26, 2009, 11:38

2010

SIXTH YEAR
SINCE FOUNDING

BE HUMBLE, BE HUMBLE

How quickly 2010 has passed. Time is relentless and waits for no one. We're focused on personnel training and making another leap forward. Perhaps there have been days that I let slip by without giving it a thought. How diligently are we seeking ways to embody 'Magnificent Yanolja,' our slogan for this year? This is a question I must continually ask myself.

Have I fully understood the nuances of Yanolja's growth? Or does it merely appear to have grown? There should be unending inquiries. The journey is underway. The silent battle for survival began days ago. How will Yanolja's personnel training system unfold? I need to earnestly reflect on how I'm using my time in 2010: am I working toward specific goals for Yanolja, or am I squandering precious moments? We must not forget that losing focus now could mean facing scarcity instead of reaping a bountiful harvest.

Be humble. Be humble.

And let's also strive to be intelligent in our approach.

Yanolja's true strength isn't centreed on me. It emerges when all Yanolja members come together, share insights and act in unison. We need a powerful collective energy. There's an urgent need for talent development, a new leap forward, and a strategy for Yanolja to become magnificent. Time is already ticking away.

January 8, 2010, 21:10

I WANT TO WELCOME DECEMBER WITH A SMILE

February has arrived. The first month of 2010 flew by, barely giving me time to reflect, and now another day, another beginning, is upon us. February is a crucial month, marked by the opening of Hotel Ellee Cheonan, the main renewal of Yanolja, and the need to find another solution to create Yanolja's unique features. The world demands that everyone hustles tirelessly. Yet, I find joy in witnessing the manifestation of Yanolja's distinct beliefs and passion.

I am confident that if the rest of 2010 unfolds like January, I will conclude the year with a smile. Metrics like performance and sales may be significant, but what truly matters is where I've invested my passion and heart. My belief in Yanolja stems from feeling and seeing that passion. February is hectic. There's the Lunar New Year, the opening of Ellee Hotel, changes to the Yanolja website, the magazine's direction, the motel business strategy, preparations for hotel reservations, and systemizing employee training.

It's a month filled with numerous tasks, making it a month of happiness. There were days when I was busy without clear direction, but now knowing precisely what needs to be done is a sign of development and growth. I hope February will be a well-led month, propelling us forward.

February 1, 2010, 01:07

LET'S THINK, DECIDE, PRACTICE
AND MAKE IT HAPPEN

When faced with obstacles or engulfed in uncertainty about the future, I continue thinking until I find a way out. Thinking has led me to where I am today. I spend all day thinking, even when answers elude me and clarity seems distant. The day I stop thinking is the day I lose my purpose.

Sometimes, answers appear unattainable. I feel like I've reached a conclusion, only to realize it's the beginning of a new train of thought, presenting yet another problem to ponder. The closer I get to a solution, the further it moves away. Therefore, I must engage in constant, comprehensive thinking, focusing on the essence, as it is a crucial step in finding answers.

This leads to practice. Practice involves transforming thoughts into tangible actions and adapting them to real-world situations. While thinking requires focus, practice is a more challenging task due to the barriers between mind, body and reality. It's like a complex assignment where easy surrender or clumsy attempts can lead to unsuccessful outcomes. Implementing ideas requires understanding their original intent and adapting them to reality. These challenges are why not everyone achieves success.

There are many challenges in the tasks we undertake. I need to live my life with constantly evolving thoughts. Through this process of thinking, I aim to become a leader who can guide with stability. It's essential to stay true to the original purpose of each thought, analysing and implementing it carefully in accordance with the actual situation. It's a demanding process, but an essential part of our responsibilities.

The culmination of thought is decision-making. We must act promptly and precisely to give tangible and valuable form to our decisions. This is crucial for survival in today's capitalist society. In the competitive world we inhabit, Yanolja is engaged in a constant battle for survival. Thoughts must lead to decisions, and practice must refine thoughts into tangible outcomes.

February 20, 2010

I WANT TO BE THE INDISPENSABLE ASSET FOR YANOLJA'S PASSION AND DREAMS

March has arrived, bringing the realization that much can change based on my pursuits. Recognizing this can be both weighty and surprising, but I am not one to shy away from it.

I frequently question whether I am worthy of being a Yanolja man. As its founder, I hold that title, but as Yanolja grows incrementally, I hope that my heart expands in tandem. I am resolved to maintain my position only as long as I continue to grow and contribute positively. I am aware of where I belong, yet I acknowledge that the moment greed creeps in, complications arise.

As Yanolja aspires to greater heights, I consider the numerous employees and affiliates whose survival, prosperity and dreams are intertwined with our company. Should greed infiltrate my heart, it would severely impede our progress. I must avoid actions driven by greed that could mar the precious value capable of yielding significant results and remarkable progress.

I am happy that Yanolja is growing in proportion to my deepening affection and contemplation for it. As time goes by, and as my thoughts for Yanolja intensify, I hope that someone will remind me to curb my greed and recall the original dream I had for Yanolja, should it ever hinder our growth.

The swift passage of time erodes my youth, and I hope to be left with memories of confidence and values rather than regrets. Yanolja has a significant journey ahead. I still aspire to be the asset that Yanolja needs to fuel its passion and dreams. We enter March 2010 with the hope that Yanolja will evolve into a truly remarkable company.

March 1, 2010, 05:07

SINCE FOUNDING YANOLJA, THERE HAS NOT BEEN A MOMENT WHEN I WAS NOT HAPPY

This year, spring seemed unusually brief, swiftly transitioning from winter into summer. As the bare branches turned lush, I've become more conscious of my own aging. Imagining my face and hands marked by deep wrinkles, I feel a compelling urge to live more purposefully.

Since founding Yanolja, there hasn't been a moment when I haven't felt happy. Reflecting on my journey, I realize that even during challenging times, I found happiness. I used to be a boy who longed for a different family background, but now I stand tall, walking proudly on my own path.

My childhood and 20s were filled with hardships. Through these trials, I learned that happiness isn't solely derived from success. True happiness comes from appreciating and harmonizing with those around me. Success is rarely a solo endeavour. Look at Yanolja – much of its value stems from people around me, not just from myself.

I don't engage in sales activities. I'm not skilled in design or planning, nor am I an engineer or adept manager. I don't have extensive experience or substantial wealth. I'm not exceptionally smart or highly educated. What I do possess is the habit of thinking constantly, a passion for Yanolja, unwavering willpower and the support of the Yanolja team.

Team leader Hwang Doo-hyeon's words, "I hope Yanolja does not succeed through the sweat and blood of others," have echoed in my mind for three days.

Initially, they upset me, but they have now transformed into a firm resolve in my heart. I am grateful for those who contribute to our comfortable lives. Happiness is not just about personal contentment; it involves creating an environment where everyone around me can thrive. This commitment is what prevents me from failing. Time is fleeting, and life has its end. Wouldn't it be wonderful to be remembered as someone who bloomed and faded beautifully?

May 19, 2010, 15:11

SECURING AND FOSTERING TALENT IS THE CEO'S JOB

The early morning air is refreshing, yet my recent nights have been restless. Despite my attempts at sound sleep, various concerns, such as my child falling ill, interrupt my rest. As the company grows and the employee count rises, the number of decisions I face increases. I am neither a genius nor a clairvoyant who can always make the right decisions. As a CEO, what must I do to make the best choices?

Since founding the company, I've been a field worker, hustling to generate sales. But my current role isn't about being in the field; it's about envisioning. My responsibility is to provide a 'direction' for our journey, not a specific 'position.' Setting practical and specific goals is a task for each team member. My role at Yanolja is to share the vision, enabling team members to set precise objectives.

We must never forget that the goal of business is success. In the capitalist market, a string of failures can lead to a company's closure. What does it take to be successful? It requires an objective analysis of the company and market, the ability to craft strategies from this analysis and effective implementation. Key to this process is having talented individuals. Therefore, my greatest duty as CEO is to secure and nurture talent.

Yanolja must become a haven for talent – a place where employees act independently, fulfil their responsibilities, receive the best compensation and take pride in their work. Achieving this will bring Yanolja even closer to success.

June 4, 2010, 05:25

I WILL DRAW A VERY BEAUTIFUL PICTURE

Like the canvas for a painting, the world presents itself to me as a space of infinite possibilities. However, the quality of my life, much like a painting, will be judged on the finesse and excellence of my skills. Some people live under the illusion that they were born with many advantages, while others lament their perceived lack of fortune. Yet, as life progresses, it becomes clear that nobody is born with inherent advantages like material wealth, personal honour, moral integrity, or familial love.

Everyone starts from zero, fairly and squarely. To believe that some start with everything while others start with nothing is to admit a lack of skill in navigating life's canvas. Life is full of variables: how to live and whom to seek as mentors. However, it's undeniable that ultimately, you decide how to lead your life and the kind of person you want to be to your family, colleagues, friends, and most importantly, to yourself.

The picture you paint of your life depends on your skills. You might be born with natural talent, but without practice, you could end up worse off than someone who has diligently honed their skills. This is a truth universally acknowledged. Life may not always be easy, and internal turmoil may arise, but you must overcome these challenges. Whether it's in business, work, family, friendship, love, wealth or fame, everything hinges on where you place your heart.

Favourable outcomes are achieved through mental discipline, patience and persistence in your convictions. Reflecting on how to control and guide your stubborn mind is essential in becoming a person of substance, with a beautiful life and a rich heart.

June 15, 2010, 11:53

I AIM TO FOCUS ALL MY EFFORTS ON WHAT I CAN DO BEST

It appears that no problem is insurmountable. Problems are likely to be resolved one way or another if approached with deep thought, time and a search for answers. Thinking is the key to gaining insights. Even if an immediate answer doesn't emerge, the process of thinking equips you with other skills necessary to devise a solution. As time moves on, I find myself in possession of more things and, therefore, more responsibilities. These range from the trivial to the extremely burdensome. The way to navigate life is rooted in this sense of responsibility. Regardless of my performance, whether poor or excellent, the outcomes will invariably reflect my life's journey.

I never want to hesitate or shift these responsibilities onto others. I sincerely hope to bear them silently, even when I feel the urge to make excuses. Isn't this the life I've chosen, or the life that I must ultimately lead? Today, as always, focusing on unresolved or uncreated tasks holds great significance and allure for me.

To truly enjoy life, I wish to find joy in thinking, rather than seeking it elsewhere. I hope to find fulfilment in creating and solving problems, and in interacting with the world. I am committed to focusing all my efforts on my strengths to live my life fully, ensuring a life that is both well-lived and worthy of being lived.

September 23, 2010, 03:35

RUSHING THROUGH LIFE
DAY-TO-DAY IS RISKY

In the face of imminent danger, abnormal signals often arise. The same holds true for Yanolja. There are signs of deviation from our intended path, yet they seem to be overlooked by those responsible. Are we neglecting to look toward the future and forgetting our fundamental purpose? The more we hasten through our daily tasks, reassuring ourselves of our hard work, the greater the risk of losing control becomes.

'Hotel reservations, social commerce, motel business, direct business division, discount cards, motel reservations' – now that these initiatives are underway, they demand results. These results stem from the process, which is rooted in our initial plans. Success comes from navigating through crises without losing sight of our true direction, even if it involves navigating through trial and error.

For 'hotel reservations,' we must consider the value that hotel reservations bring. Are we adhering to a process aligned with our original plan? Success relies on each member pondering what's best.

With 'social commerce, couple ticket,' starting with the assumption that things will naturally go well can lead to a rude awakening. The market is challenging, and ultimately, it's the customers who determine what's valuable.

Efforts to release products on time are commendable, but hastily launching a subpar product is a recipe for failure. Imagine the repercussions of selling undercooked rice because of impatience. In social commerce, with a model that thrives on word-of-mouth, negative feedback can be as impactful as the positive. Operating with a 'sell first, think later' approach is a path to failure.

For 'motel business, direct business division, discount cards, motel reservations,' complacency or lack of direction, even during successful periods, can lead to accidents or loss of focus. Hard work alone is not sufficient, especially when the team expands. Without a clear direction or understanding of tasks, even collective efforts of many can lead to failure.

I am confident in Yanolja's success, but survival comes first. Various warning signals indicate potential dangers. To achieve success, we must hold onto our initial goals and direction.

November 7, 2010, 11:51

Over the past ten years, Yanolja has undertaken countless initiatives, not all of which were successful. Our growth has been shaped significantly by several failures. Among these, two projects stand out as particularly painful: the social commerce business 'Couple Ticket' and the hotel reservation service 'Hotel Grab.'

'Couple Ticket' was initiated using the content from Yanolja's dating course service 'Date&.' At that time, social commerce was burgeoning, led by the rise of Ticket Monster. We entered the market with a unique 'dating' concept. However, the market rapidly became oversaturated, with more than 500 social commerce services emerging almost overnight. Struggling to secure low-cost, high-quality products and attract customers, we saw no viable reason or will to continue the project. We terminated the service sooner than many others. Although it was a hard pill to swallow, it was prudent to conclude the project swiftly. Lingering on in hope would have led to greater losses.

In contrast to 'Couple Ticket,' 'Hotel Grab' continued for over five years. Before transitioning to 'Yanolja Hotel Comparison,' 'Hotel Grab' failed to produce notable results for a lengthy period. Despite not generating significant sales, we should have carved out a market niche with specialized services. Instead, the business meandered on with unclear expectations. The team members faced challenges and, organizationally, we must critically reflect on our failure to dedicate full efforts to enhancing the service.

These experiences, though fraught with difficulty, have been essential in shaping Yanolja's journey and learning process.

I WANT TO BE A PROTECTING FENCE EVEN IN THE BATTLEFIELD

Early morning, December 19. With less than 15 days left in the year, I reflect on how swiftly time has passed. The year seemed to breeze by, but it was filled with many events and milestones. Time seems to pause momentarily, yet it flows on uninterrupted. Although I feel as young as ever, I'm now in my mid-30s, and it's been six years since I founded the company.

I sense my mind evolving alongside my aging body. It's essential for me to learn patience, curb my impatience and eschew greed. I must distinguish between what I can give and what I can gain, striving for clarity in my actions and decisions.

Welcoming each new year in better shape than the last is both a blessing and a privilege. Despite the harshness of modern society, I envision Yanolja as a nurturing fence, offering protection and solace rather than contributing to the callous environment.

Challenges are an inherent part of new ventures, often fraught with effort and sacrifice. Yet, without embracing these challenges, the future becomes daunting, filled with uncertainty. If we fail to find the proverbial 'water of life,' each passing year will bring Yanolja closer to darkness and despair.

This is why many companies continuously seek new ventures. We must avoid greed but also shun laziness. Our focus should be unwavering, regardless of the task at hand, proceeding step-by-step. Only by clearly identifying what Yanolja and I need to do, and diligently working toward these goals, can we truly enjoy the holiday season in peace.

None of the projects we initiated in 2010 have yet reached completion. However, I am confident that ultimately, we will see them stand independently and successfully. With fewer than 15 days remaining in the year, I feel a sense of gratitude toward Yanolja. This year has been a significant and challenging one for the company, a year marked by good battles. I know that next year will present another set of battles in the harsh realities of modern society.

It is my responsibility and duty to ensure that the perseverance and victories of all Yanolja members are not in vain, but rather lead to outcomes that bring peace and stability.

December 19, 2010, 02:27

2011
SEVENTH YEAR
SINCE FOUNDING

THE MORE THE COMPANY SCALES UP, THE MORE WE SHOULD REMAIN ALERT

At Yanolja, I constantly remind our employees to stay alert in their work. As the one setting this standard, it's crucial for me to lead by example and be the epitome of alertness. For various reasons, the first quarter is particularly critical for the company. It's a period when we're likely to experience heightened financial pressures. Last year, we saw a significant increase in sales, and I am proud of the battles we fought and won.

It's vital to remember that our expenditures have risen alongside our sales. Achieving our 2011 goals requires careful management of spending. A company's ability to make new investments hinges on a delicate balance between sales and expenses. While we cannot afford to halt investments – they are the engines of future growth – we must remember that investments also mean expenditures. Successfully navigating this quarter will depend on our ability to walk the tightrope between prudence and audacity.

As the company grows, the risks amplify. We must never forget that unchecked scaling up can lead to dire mistakes. Yanolja needs to evolve into a company that can fortify itself against future crises by establishing a robust financial structure. The groundwork for further growth starts this quarter, and we are already being put to the test. We must resist complacency and maintain constant vigilance.

January 7, 2011, 02:09

I START FEBRUARY 1 WITH THE HOPE TO BE SMILING ON MARCH 1

It's already February 1, and one month of the year has swiftly passed by. As I look back, I contemplate the significance of my presence during this time. Reflection often brings to light shortcomings and regrets, while looking forward conjures a mix of fear and hope.

The present is a crossroads where the past and future intersect. In today's society, the notion of living in the present for its own sake seems long lost. Today's joys, actions and emotions are often overshadowed by future aspirations. The present has become a time to relentlessly forge ahead, setting aside everything in pursuit of what lies ahead.

Only as we approach life's end does our focus shift from the future back to the past, as we sort through regrets and reminisce about days gone by. I acknowledge this tendency in myself, and as days, months, and years fleetingly pass, it becomes evident that my youth is behind me.

Perhaps it's time to relinquish the notion that I still possess the passion of my 20s, even ceasing to imagine that I retain a 20-something's heart. It seems appropriate now to explore the depths of what my 30s have to offer. Now, as a father, the need for maturity beckons, and with age comes the necessity for deeper contemplation.

Thus begins my February 1. My hope is to greet March 1 with a smile, moving beyond January's regrets or achievements, ensuring that February is a month dedicated to earnest preparation for March.

February 1, 2011, 03:12

I'LL DO WHAT I CAN, NOT WHAT I CAN'T

It's time to rest. Upon waking in the morning, I'll revisit the path I must take, contemplating it thoroughly. This introspection is crucial and aligns with what I do best. While there are many things beyond my capabilities, I choose not to dwell on those limitations. Instead, I focus on the one thing I can do well, pouring my passion into it.

That's the essence of who I am. The journey may be lengthy, but my commitment is to persevere until the end. This steadfast approach has been, and will continue to be, a pivotal factor in my success. My thoughts are magical and precious, uplifting and guiding me. I must never cease to think, constantly re-evaluating and determining my course of action. That is my mission.

February 10, 2011, 01:51

LET'S CHOOSE GROWTH
WITHOUT FEARING PAIN

"What will I live by?"

This question has been echoing in my mind. It's a day for profound reflection on my existence, my identity, and my future.

What should I live by and how can I live well?

These questions have long preoccupied my thoughts. How should I shape Yanolja's future? What form will Yanolja take in the years ahead? These aren't just fleeting queries; they're profound reflections on the essence of my life, the value of Yanolja, the significance of my family, and the value of my colleagues. Why must I ponder so deeply on these matters? Ultimately, they encompass my life, the journey I traverse, and the outcomes for which I am accountable.

Do I live in apprehension of this reality? Whenever doubt creeps in, I sometimes wonder if I'm presuming that I can handle everything, akin to self-administering painkillers to dull the discomfort.

"What should I live by?"

As someone in my position, there's a temptation to focus only on what benefits me, but that is far from straightforward. Even I sometimes struggle with this question. I could ask those around me who might view my role as mere vanity, but ultimately, this is my life. It's up to me to seek answers and make decisions.

The truths that spur my growth also inflict inner pain, but pain is an inherent part of growth. With this knowledge, I consciously choose a path of growth over the fear of pain. They say that merely sustaining what you have is doing well, but without growth, even maintenance is unattainable. Therefore, my choice is clear: to control myself, willingly embrace the pain that fosters growth, and evolve through it.

March 6, 2011, 22:14

LET'S MOVE OUT OF THE COMFORT ZONE, EMBRACE FEAR AND START THE ENGINE

Stepping out of the comfort zone invites fear, but such a step is crucial for progress. It means choosing to confront fear. My mind craves comfort, yet my nature yearns to chase new ventures. This dichotomy often leads to hesitation, but ultimately, I opt for the new challenges that come with fear rather than remaining in the safety of the familiar.

Today, a relentless headache plagued me, a physical manifestation of a day spent in busy idleness. It's been a taxing day, weighing heavily on my body, mind and spirit, even though I've accomplished little. It's a day of internal struggle between the allure of comfort and the prodding of fear urging me to aim higher. Quick solutions elude me, but I hope that whatever choice I make, it propels me beyond my limits, igniting me like a flame.

I step into an uncertain future, hoping for the wisdom to embrace the rough tension and potential dangers rather than succumb to lethargic peace. Why must I disrupt my tranquility and risk it all? This question haunts me, yet it's a day where I have no choice but to break from peace and embrace risk. When the day calls for words, thoughts, and actions to transcend their nascent stage and crystallize into reality, can I muster the courage to risk again? Despite my foolish, trivial questions, the answer is clear. Embracing tension and fear as a young individual isn't too daunting. It is, in fact, preparation for the future. Time to start the engine.

March 16, 2011, 01:12

WE OFTEN FORGET THE VALUE OF THE MINUTE THAT JUST PASSED BY

The contradiction between not wanting to live in vain and the inability to fulfil that desire is a common struggle. We can't reclaim the past, and the future remains unknown. Often, we fail to recognize the significance of a minute that has just gone by. Despite the finite nature of time, we sometimes live as if it's infinite, unaware of the shame and emptiness in living without purpose.

I constantly demand action from myself, yet these demands feel like fleeting promises, leaving me burdened with the sense that I'm navigating life without direction. I'm uncertain about the future, regretful of the past and complacent in the present. Time slips away, leaving me with nothing substantial... I hope my whole life doesn't unfold in such a manner.

May 11, 2011, 00:21

WHAT YOU DO TODAY BECOMES
THE SEED OF TOMORROW

"One is followed by two, two by three, three by four, and four by ... ?"

With the completion of one project, many others arise, each growing in scope and complexity. Therefore, I can't tackle everything alone; I need to find capable individuals. This challenge extends beyond personal leadership to encompass each team's operational style and the broader societal structure.

I used to think completing one project would settle things, but each success leads to new, larger tasks. Development means a steadily increasing workload. The outcome hinges on how well tasks are carried out and whether we advance or remain stagnant. Everything in my present is a result of small actions I took in the past – the result of seeds that have now grown and demand my attention.

Ultimately, it's up to me to conclude these tasks and seek new or improved paths. As I often remind myself, today is the seed of tomorrow. Embracing this responsibility is challenging, yet it is wiser to lead proactively than be passively pulled through life.

June 14, 2011, 00:31

I DON'T KNOW HOW FAR I'LL GO,
BUT I'LL SPEED UP

Despite recognizing my slowing pace, I find myself unable to shed heavy burdens; instead, I keep taking on even heavier loads. I'm pushing my employees to accelerate as well. This makes me feel irresponsible, as I declare everything to be important, while knowing deep down that if everything is deemed important, ultimately nothing is.

As the representative of the company, do I possess clear standards and direction for the current situation? Yanolja is growing larger, yet it feels like a company whose control box is malfunctioning. Its growth rate is decelerating, and the path to revival seems elusive. What is the state of Yanolja in 2011?

People often ask, "Isn't that enough?" or "Why continue? How much more do you want?" Yet, I'm not content. Had my motivation been solely financial, I would have ceased my efforts long ago. But my drive to progress persists. I am determined to reinvigorate Yanolja, which seems to have slowed down like a slug, and to reignite its momentum. I am uncertain how far Yanolja will go, but I am confident it will find its path and gain speed once more. However, the questions of "with what?" and "how?" may take time to resolve. I will continue to ponder deeply, believing that overcoming this challenge will lead to the answers I seek.

July 26, 2011, 00:55

CONTINUOUS SUCCESS, NOT A ONE-TIME ACHIEVEMENT, IS TRUE SUCCESS

Occasionally, I find myself racing toward immediate results. However, reaching a result is not the finale. Whether the outcome is favourable or not, the journey doesn't end there. After each result, it's essential to return to the starting line and strive for the next goal. This continuous cycle is the essence of life.

I once believed that a single instance of success was sufficient, but I am gradually learning that true success is a persistent state, lasting until life's end. While it's acknowledged that I have achieved something in the past, I view it not as the culmination but a foundation for greater opportunities, and a more robust starting point for future endeavours.

Today is not the conclusion. It's important to realize that survival hinges on competing for another tomorrow. These words are penned today to contemplate if there is indeed an endpoint to success.

September 11, 2011, 01:55

AT THE YEAR'S END, I FEEL BOTH OVERWHELMED AND AFRAID

Life is a blend of acknowledging the past, envisioning the future, aging and finding reasons to live. As the year draws to a close, I am simultaneously exhilarated and apprehensive.

It's time to reflect on what has guided my life and whether I've lived well. The pride I feel in these reflections becomes my benchmark for a well-lived life. But what about when I feel unsettled or anxious? At each year's end, I question whether I can consider it a good year by my standards, not by others', and gauge the depth of my contemplations.

What will guide me in the coming year? I've journeyed too far to let time slip by thoughtlessly. Ultimately, I am propelled forward, my mind filled with thoughts of the past and the future. Yet, I am determined to stand steadfast in my life. While I cannot be completely satisfied with everything – my company, my family, my life – I refuse to cease my efforts to have a meaningful impact. Thus, I must contemplate what will shape my essence.

December 30, 2011

2012
EIGHTH YEAR
SINCE FOUNDING

A TIME TO DRAW A LONG-TERM PICTURE, NOT A SHORT-TERM ONE

The allure of something new is always invigorating. As one year ends and another commences, my mind is preoccupied with perfecting ongoing projects rather than embarking on entirely new ventures. This year, I aspire to ignite a renewed passion for existing projects, recognizing that life isn't always about pursuing novelty. Perhaps, as we age, our focus naturally shifts toward seeing through the commitments we already hold.

I find myself at a juncture in life where drawing a long-term plan becomes more critical than chasing short-term goals. Realizing this, I am inclined to embrace aging not with melancholy but with a resolve to exercise greater self-control and remain open to change. The year 2011 was eventful, and now, the responsibility lies with me to complete and nurture the initiatives I've started. This represents a new challenge and a step toward solidifying Yanolja's foundation of stability. Let us once again stride forward and sing the hymn of hope.

January 2, 2012, 07:55

WHEN MARCH ARRIVES AFTER WINTER, I FEEL LIKE GOING TO WAR

With the departure of winter, March arrives. Each year, this month feels like a battlefield. As 2012 unfolds, I'm curious about the challenges this March will bring. Yanolja has now reached its seventh anniversary. These years have brought significant transformations, both personally and within the company. I am deeply thankful for these positive changes. The person I am today and the results Yanolja has achieved are the culmination of days filled with effort. Though still in a nascent stage and not yet complete, I am confident that Yanolja will celebrate many more anniversaries – the tenth, 20th, and even the 100th – as long as we continue to infuse each day with passion.

Let's embark.

Let's forge ahead.

With unyielding passion in our hearts.

If we maintain this momentum, the future of Yanolja will undoubtedly become steadfast.

March 2, 2012, 12:49

LET'S START ADDING ONE AT A TIME, STARTING AT ZERO

The sky today is exceptionally clear, heralding the approaching summer, yet in my mind, it already feels like autumn and winter. Time seems to be slipping away. It feels imperative to grasp at least one substantial achievement. Being busy is often seen as positive, but it can also mean overlooking many things. It's time to adopt a mindset of starting anew from zero, carefully building step-by-step. This approach could prevent future challenges. The clarity of the summer sky, resembling that of fall, invites reflection and future planning. But reflections must lead to action. My focus for the remainder of 2012 is to tighten the loose ends of ongoing tasks and commit to learning and growing. By replacing idleness with thoughtful action and leaving no gaps, I can find new breakthroughs and continue to evolve.

June 27, 2012, 13:54

I COMMIT MYSELF TO MY 'INITIAL DETERMINATION'

It's been some time since my last entry. The past month has whirled by in such a frenzy that finding moments to write has been a challenge, despite my intermittent musings marked by happiness, melancholy, concerns and hopes.

I am often struck by unexpected occurrences that prompt reflection and action. There are moments when I long for consistency, yet I also recognize the tedium that might accompany such predictability.

People often ask, "How are you doing these days?" Reflecting on this, as autumn unfolds and a time for harvesting approaches, my thoughts turn to both this year's yield and planning for the next. Despite perceptions of my financial wellbeing, the reality is a daily preoccupation with financial concerns, alongside health worries. There are days when the desire for respite is overwhelming, yet work beckons. A major undertaking lies ahead with organizational restructuring, and I face the personal challenge of learning English.

However, my most significant endeavour is recommitting to my initial resolve. This is where my current state lies – in contemplation and action. After navigating a significant storm, I sometimes fear that arrogance has crept in, rendering everything mundane and trivial. I await the subsiding of this arrogance, yet it persists stubbornly. I conclude this entry without definitive answers, hoping that future writings might provide some. As October progresses, I think my reflections will deepen.

October 8, 2012, 00:36

THE IMPORTANCE OF KNOWING YOURSELF BETTER THAN OTHERS

Prioritizing self-awareness is essential in life, and this especially holds true for leaders. A leader is scrutinized, not just internally but also by others. I never view such scrutiny negatively. External and internal checks can serve as a guiding force, aligning and recalibrating my path.

We often act based on our heart's judgment rather than our head's, as our heart is the chief commander within us. Fortunately, I have the gift of self-awareness, sensing my heart's inclinations before they become apparent to others. Recognizing oneself first is a significant advantage, yet we frequently overlook this benefit.

What I am aware of now will eventually become known to others. While it may seem exclusive knowledge at first, the truth is that it eventually becomes common. This fact often slips my mind. Whether as a leader or not, our lives are continuously exposed to others. Coexistence inevitably leads to sharing our actions, words, form, work, and thoughts, and even our hearts. Isn't this the reality we all live in? This exposure is even more pronounced in a leadership role. If one controls their life solely for personal gain, it is unlikely that others will respect or accept them as a leader.

Some might think being a boss merely involves having money or being the one who pays salaries on time. I question this view. Is a boss simply someone with money, a title and the ability to pay wages? I don't think so. A true boss needs to be open, accountable and understand their purpose. Hiding, focusing only on validating others, or reducing their role to a salary distributor diminishes their ability to lead effectively. This is my understanding of what it means to be a boss and, by extension, my view of life itself.

I know how easily I can deceive myself. The human mind, inherently weak and impressionable, often struggles with maintaining self-confidence. It's crucial for me to consistently monitor how I manage myself and prioritize presenting myself as a responsible individual, rather than focusing solely on how others perceive me. We are neither Taoists nor deities; living a life completely satisfied with every aspect is unrealistic.

Like everyone else, I have my priorities, but aiming for near-perfect satisfaction in what matters most is essential. If one strives to be completely content in all areas of life, it defeats the purpose of living. I don't aspire to be a Taoist or a deity, but rather, I wish to live a normal, happy life. However, at Yanolja, being 'normal' isn't an option for me. As a leader, it is my responsibility to act, communicate and share a vision. This role is a choice I made, and it holds great value and significance for me. That's why aspiration is crucial.

The way I am seen, heard, discussed, contemplated, and envisioned by Yanolja's employees, partner companies, and clients deeply matters. If I were to take a passive stance, I could simply remain a person of wealth and a shareholder. However, as the head of Yanolja, I have consciously placed myself in this role. My actions now represent not just myself, but the entire Yanolja team. The outward image I project is a reflection of my inner self, yet it also significantly affects the entire organization. With this in mind, how can I afford to neglect self-management?

Greed holds significant importance in my life. It's a part of human nature to prioritize oneself, and I'm no exception. Over a decade of running a company has taught me that while greed may seem beneficial in the short term, it ultimately doesn't serve Yanolja's interests and could backfire. This realization has led me to a life of constant self-reprimand and correction, especially when greed takes over or I feel on the verge of collapse.

But does this self-awareness make me a virtuous person? Not necessarily. There are still moments when I falter, lose my composure, and struggle to maintain self-discipline. Upholding integrity and doing the right thing is challenging. I often oscillate between focusing on tasks and taking breaks to escape the tediousness. Yet, I find myself continually returning to a state of self-recognition, striving to understand my true desires.

I don't aim for perfection in self-management – that would be exhausting. However, I believe it's crucial to recognize when greed becomes overwhelming or when lethargy sets in. It's about finding the right balance – knowing when to exert effort and when to relax. This approach helps maintain a steady rhythm in life without losing direction.

Even outside the realm of business, self-management is vital. If your mind is unfocused, your activities suffer. Poor health hinders your ability to act, lack of knowledge in your field limits recognition, and without companionship, life becomes lonely. Ultimately, effective self-management lays the foundation for a fulfiling life.

Am I managing myself well these days? My hope is that both I and we can periodically self-evaluate, ensuring we live as conscientious human beings.

THE END OF A YEAR IS ALWAYS FOLLOWED BY THE BEGINNING OF A NEW ONE

On days like today, I find myself intensely curious, almost to the point of frenzy. Ultimately, I realize that the answers to how I've lived my life will come only with time. Instead of trying to predict the future, I choose to simply live. The end of one year seamlessly transitions into the beginning of another, illustrating how beginnings and endings are interconnected. Just like everyone else, I exist within this cyclical flow of time. This realization compels me to carefully consider what will cultivate a fulfiling life.

It's crucial for me to manage my desires and greed effectively. There's a worry that constantly nags at me — the fear that joy and happiness might be eroded by uncontrolled desires and greed, leaving a life consumed solely by these insatiable urges. I hope to avoid such a fate, falling into the trap of perpetual dissatisfaction despite abundant wealth. May I never lose sight of the essence of living a meaningful life. I aspire to be a wise person who not only lives thoughtfully but also deeply contemplates the purpose and direction of life.

December 24, 2012

2013

NINTH YEAR
SINCE FOUNDING

YOU LIVE ONLY ONCE,
NOT TWICE OR THRICE

In life, we are faced with numerous choices, both significant and minor. Ultimately, these choices are personal
– they belong to us and not to others. Believing in the
choices we make is essential for a fulfiling life. I often
consider the idea of having the authority to make my
own choices, rather than being subject to the decisions of
others or feeling compelled to choose. Whether it's about
love, work, life, health, time, or relationships, wouldn't it
be better to be the one actively making these choices?

Many people relinquish this authority too readily. Even
when beneficial opportunities present themselves, a slight
error in judgment can render these opportunities inacces-
sible. People become accustomed to this, believing it's their
fate, convincing themselves it's easier to be chosen than to
choose. But is this the case? Making choices is undoubtedly
challenging and accompanied by immense responsibility.

But do we live twice, or thrice? Isn't each moment we
have uniquely irreplaceable? To live a life that's truly our
own, we must constantly dream, deliberate and grapple with challenges. Accepting the reality of unlimited
responsibilities and obligations is part of moving forward. I constantly remind myself that while everyone
dreams of success, not all achieve it. To lead a life of your
own choosing, it's crucial to manage and endure even the
smallest emotional impulses of the moment. Sometimes,
this means deferring immediate gratification. This discipline is the foundation of making meaningful choices.

There is still much for me to achieve. I often find
myself succumbing to the allure of immediate pleasures

when making decisions. Yet, shouldn't I aim to exhibit patience at least 51% of the time? I am convinced that if I manage to exercise restraint more than half the time, at least half of my life will be on the path to success. How far are you prepared to go in making your own choices? Implementing this willpower, I believe, is the essence of mastering one's life.

I aspire to be strict with myself to achieve success, to be kind to others and appreciate the beauty of life, and to show love to my family and spread affection in my life. If I aim for these goals 51% of the time, then there will be only 49% left for regret. Ultimately, the person who makes choices is the one who gets chosen.

February 15, 2013, 09:48

NOW IS THE TIME TO MAKE US, NOT ME, STRONG

It's the first Monday of March, a time that always takes me back to the early days of our company. Back then, it was a challenging period filled only with dreams. Questions like "What should I live for?", "Who will I become?" and "How should I lead?" were unanswered in my mind. Eight years ago, the path ahead was unclear, the company was unformed, and potential employees hesitated to join us. But how do I find myself now, eight years later? Thankfully, I'm beginning to understand what I'm living for and am forming a vision of who I want to be. I'm recognizing what needs to be done, and it's a relief not to feel stuck in the same place I was eight years ago, not blaming others or the world for my circumstances.

I wonder if I should be more nervous and concerned about my perspective on the future, my life and everything around me. The days when I was the only hard worker and believed I was the only one capable of certain tasks are gone. There are now more things beyond my individual capacity than within it. This signifies that Yanolja's destiny is no longer in my hands alone. I am no longer the sole guarantor of its future. The company has evolved past the point where its fate is tied to the owner's habits and thoughts. It has become an entity that requires collective thought and effort. Our reality now demands that every team member acknowledges their role in steering the company and acts accordingly, with a clear understanding of their individual contributions.

Yanolja recently celebrated its eighth anniversary. Eight years ago, I was preoccupied with surviving each day rather than planning for the future. But now, the focus has shifted toward contemplating our team's future and exploring new paths. I aspire to gift Yanolja with growth, focusing on "What will make us, the Yanolja team, strong?" rather than just "What will make me strong?"

March 4, 2013, 15:12

THE MORE INTENSE MY FEARS
AND THE GRAVER THE SITUATION,
THE STRONGER MY RESOLVE BECOMES

The hungrier I am, the harder I try to survive. The more intense my fears and the graver the situation, the stronger my resolve becomes. Today seems to be one of those days when this sentiment rings especially true. On such days, I reflect on passion. Instead of dwelling on how well I have done or am doing, my focus needs to be on acting with dynamic passion.

The future is inevitable. What kind of future will we choose to embrace? We must remember that our present actions are shaping that future.

March 27, 2013, 01:18

LET'S NOT INSIST THAT I'M THE CENTRE OF EVERYTHING

There was a time when I wished time would fly. Those were my days of immaturity and ignorance. Eager to escape the days of hardship, I hoped for better times. Reflecting on those times now, I see my substantial progress. I have a nice car, quality clothes, a commendable job, and I'm a business owner. It's not just about the money; I no longer face the struggles of washing with ice-cold water in winter or waking at dawn to change coal briquettes for heat.

Ice-cold water, coal briquettes – it sounds almost foreign, but that was my reality. My body was all I had, my sole asset in the struggle for survival. How desperately did I wish for the days of hunger to pass, for a better life to dawn? Looking back, I realize there's one reason I became a business owner: Trust. I placed trust in myself, my clients, and those around me. Not everyone was satisfied, of course, but universal, reasonable trust was always my guide, never veering into excessive greed.

Today, Sujin Lee has made it. But people only see the successful version of me, not the one who endured and struggled. This is the sweetness of success. But ultimately, Sujin Lee, the person, needs more sincerity for the future than pretense for the present. That realization hit me suddenly. I've made it, yes, but how long will it last? Therefore, I understand: Let's not pretend to be the centre of everything.

June 6, 2013, 02:13

PASSION MUST HAVE THE NOBILITY OF NOT GIVING UP

The passion of youth is mostly audacity. Youth can be crazy because of its passionate nature. I wonder if this still holds true for today's youth. At least in my time, this was the case. People often referred to it as audacity ... true passion must embody the nobility of not giving up. One must continually act with fervour. However, the passion of youth is often too easily forsaken, which is why it is often labelled as mere audacity. Whether it remains as audacity or evolves into passion is determined by someone's realization, and it only becomes the beautiful passion of youth when one acknowledges it within themselves.

People aspire to be rich, yet often relinquish this goal. Is this aspiration less common nowadays? There was a time when the whole nation was abuzz with the ambition of wealth, engaging in robust activities, strategies, and tactics. However, as society predominantly offered opportunities to large corporations, the yearning shifted to securing a good job, and emphasizing qualifications on resumes. Nowadays, however, large corporations are said to prioritize 'personality' in their hiring criteria.

Wanting to be rich but perceiving it as unattainable, people avoid voicing this ambition and instead fervently focus on securing positions in large corporations, labelling themselves as passionate youth. A country thrives when it has many youths aspiring to wealth, and a country is powerful when it can provide such opportunities. At Yanolja, we aim to be a robust company that aids young people aspiring to wealth by providing them with opportunities.

Happiness is paramount. Everyone claims that happiness is their priority, though some prioritize love. However, I assert that these priorities are fleeting. What brings happiness? Unless one retreats to a monastery for ascetic practices, we must live as part of society. Most of modern society operates under capitalism, which I regard as a chosen system.

Whether in jungle tribes or affluent America, some are wealthy while others are impoverished. Some are happy, while others experience unhappiness. While it's not a universal rule, it's worth thinking about which conditions better sustain happiness and love. We shouldn't just react negatively but objectively consider what can maintain our happiness.

To avoid mere audacity, let's critically assess if we harbour a passionate nobility of perseverance within us.

July 16, 2013, 00:24

LET ME BE ACKNOWLEDGED BY MYSELF, NOT BY OTHERS

I don't claim to grasp the meaning of life, nor am I any longer at an age where I can solely rely on the fervour of youth. As a father to a seven-year-old and a four-year-old, I have a significant journey ahead in this role. I'm past the age for concerning myself primarily with love and relationships, and I have too many responsibilities to consider starting anything new. It's an age where shouldering everything feels burdensome, yet it's too early to set it all aside.

My days seem to be a cycle, akin to life continually turning in circles. I haven't even reached the midpoint of my life, but I'm already burdened with many responsibilities. I'm striving to enhance the value of what I possess. Occasionally, though, I find myself asking, "Why?" Reflecting on my youth, I realize that today is more youthful than tomorrow. Am I living merely to reach death, or am I living to truly experience life? Everyone is destined to die, but how should I live so that, at the end of my life, I can confidently say I lived it well?

When I feel constricted by my age, the solution seems to be to move forward with passion. Rather than seeking tangible gains, I should focus on daily progression. Eventually, there will come a time for more leisurely reflection. I hope to be able to assure myself, "I am living well now. I have lived well so far." There's something more pressing than wondering what I'm living for. Perhaps what's most crucial is if my soul can ultimately be my ally. Even if I lead a life that seems absurd, my aim should be to live in a manner where I can acknowledge myself.

My objective is not to seek validation from others but to earn it from myself. As I add more years and experiences, both my achievements and shortcomings will accumulate to eventually form what I can term as the 'result.' Eventually, I'll be able to assess whether I've lived a fulfiling life or not.

Today's a new day. Running in the morning has left my mind feeling refreshed. This clarity enhances my thought process. In recent days, I've been contemplating the theme of my life. I think now is the time to set aside these reflections and charge forward again. The conclusion seems to be that I'm still at an age where definitive answers are elusive. Therefore, it appears I need to continue pressing forward to discover them.

August 11, 2013, 08:56

LET'S MAKE TIME OUR ALLY,
NOT A MONSTER

The time to wrap up 2013 and prepare for 2014 has arrived. It's uncertain whether time is our ally or a huge monster waiting to devour us. Either way, we must be prepared, hoping it turns out to be on our side. Thus, I'm faced with the need to make decisions once more. My single thought could mark the beginning of our organization's future. Therefore, I cannot take it lightly.

My mind has already moved beyond 2013, transitioning into 2014. "What are our tasks for 2014?" "What must we do?" These questions are likely to occupy my mind until the year's end. As always, I hope to find answers through deep thought. Let's think diligently.

September 12, 2013, 14:30

* During this period, I started to waver. This time marked the beginning of my journey toward stepping down as CEO in 2014. The organization felt overwhelming, and I believed I had reached the limits of my ability and confidence to lead.

THE CRITERIA FOR TODAY'S CHOICES SHOULD BE SET IN THE FUTURE

Life constantly presents us with choices, ranging from the very easy to the extremely difficult. I find myself living amid these choices, from minor daily ones to those capable of altering my life.

"Did I make the right choice today?"

Though I've known since childhood that choices carry responsibilities, I sometimes wonder if I prioritize immediate comfort over future value. Am I choosing short-term ease at the expense of potential long-term difficulties? The past is unchangeable. What's the point in dwelling on days gone by? The present is fleeting, but the future still offers opportunities. There's hope that the forthcoming days can be different, depending on how I live.

Choices entail responsibility. I believe the burden of these responsibilities lessens when choices favour future benefits over immediate gains. Each choice I make is my responsibility, aimed at ensuring the future well-being of the many members of Yanolja.

October 12, 2013, 02:56

2014
TENTH YEAR
SINCE FOUNDING

IF YOU HAVE SUBJECTIVITY,
YOU CAN RISE AGAIN LIKE A WEEBLE

Can a person always stand upright? There are days when we sway like reeds, forgetting what we should hold dear in our hearts. Am I feeling pity for my past self? Am I exhausted from being a CEO? Or do I acknowledge my lack of ability? Being shaken empties my heart. It's not a lack of confidence that causes the wavering, but rather the overwhelming thought of having to grit my teeth and forge ahead again. Knowing that I must see things through once I start is burdensome, because I constantly push myself to extremes.

People describe me as tenacious and diligent, someone who immerses themselves deeply into things with an obsessive fervour. On the other hand, they also say I possess a sensitive side and an inexplicable pathos. As a CEO, or simply as an individual, I have duties to fulfil. Sometimes I must continue despite knowing something is wrong, or I feel pressured to do even better when things are going well. These moments make it hard to just enjoy business. During periods of uncertainty, I sometimes yearn to lay down my duties. When reckless dedication gives way to such times, I put everything aside and poignantly look back at the past.

My growth to this point brings tears to my eyes. Knowing that many people around me care for me and their individual stories also touches my heart. The past years had their pain. The absence of my parents left an unfilled void in my heart, and my grandmother's death during my childhood was also deeply affecting. There were also times of turmoil during my business journey. Among these, 2014 was the most painful and challenging year, a time of significant turning points.

As 2013 ended, Yanolja appeared to be on a growth trajectory, yet internally, it seemed as if we had reached a standstill. Despite the hard work of our employees, there was a noticeable decline in efficiency. I couldn't shake off the feeling that our expansion wasn't a result of our own initiatives but rather an outcome of being swept along by the industry's momentum. Doubts crept in, making me question whether our success was merely a stroke of timely fortune and whether I lacked the capability to navigate this market structure.

These contemplations intensified as the year-end neared. Subsequently, in 2014, I made a decisive move to maintain my formal title as Yanolja's registered CEO but relinquish my operational responsibilities as the chief executive. This decision stemmed from my self-assessment, not external pressure. I grappled with feelings of inadequacy and perceived myself as an ineffective figurehead. Recognizing my limitations in fostering innovation and improvement within the organization as CEO, I concluded that my continued presence in the role was untenable.

That year marked the inception of a professional management framework at Yanolja. As 2013 ended, we sought to bolster our professional ethos by recruiting external executive officers for the first time. Among the new Chief Financial Officers we brought on board, one assumed the CEO role, while the other provided support as CFO. My cofounder and vice president were assigned the CEO role of a subsidiary, and our service director, who had been instrumental in Yanolja's journey since 2006, took on the CEO position of a newly-established entity, Yanolja Pension.

Consequently, Yanolja underwent a comprehensive organizational restructuring. I stepped aside, allowing the company's transformative growth. For nine years, my focus had been unwaveringly fixated on Yanolja, irrespective of the outcome. I stepped down without allowing time for reconsideration, either by myself or by others. This decision was accompanied by a sense of emptiness, sorrow, and apprehension. I contemplated the future, considering a year-long break to explore foreign countries with my family, to refresh my mind and immerse myself in diverse cultures.

From the moment I decided to step down from managing the company, I essentially stopped working. I was concerned, but I believed that someone more educated and professional would lead Yanolja toward innovation. Looking back, I wonder if I was fleeing from my own life. The period when I relinquished my role as CEO was when I briefly forgot that I was the master of my life. It was a time when I left everything to others in the naïve hope that they'd handle it well. It was also when I faced the greatest internal turmoil and challenges since I founded Yanolja.

It conjured a memory of the emptiness I felt when my grandmother passed. At the time, I existed in a daze, without a sense of purpose. I lost both my father and my mother at a young age, and not having them around me was not a cause of great pain, albeit a cause of resentment, because it happened before I developed my self-identity. However, losing my grandmother was profoundly painful for me. When I left Yanolaja, I was as hurt and tormented during this period as I was when my grandmother passed away.

The professional management system lasted only six months. Since turning from a deficit to a profit during the early days of the company, we had never experienced a monthly loss. However, in the first half of 2014, the profit margin decreased month by month, eventually leading to losses. The internal organization was in disarray, with employees unclear about their roles or the results they should be producing. Everyone was engaged in tasks that were far removed from their original roles.

The problem wasn't with the professional management; it was with me. It was my mistake, my negligence, and my avoidance. I appointed professional managers with the intention of resetting horizons and starting afresh. Instead, however, the organization devolved into power struggles, with more focus on internal politics than actual work. Rather than self-promotion, the culture shifted to criticizing and undermining others, transforming the organization into a place of conflict and negativity. Not a day went by without some kind of incident, leading to a tumultuous internal environment. All of this was a result of my failure to properly oversee things and my evasion of responsibilities.

This crisis marked the greatest turmoil of my life, forcing me to a halt. During my six months of stepping back, I realized what had been unsettling me: a feeling of defeat or a loss of self-agency. I needed to rise again, like a Weeble. I understood that the organization couldn't be shaped or run by others. I had to personally go through the process to achieve the desired outcomes. I feared that if I continued to let things be, Yanolja, which I had built with care and dedication over the years, would crumble. I needed to become more analytical. With an indomitable spirit, I had to put an end to my brief period of disorientation. I returned to Yanolja to reorganize the team and redefine our future vision. I confronted numerous long-standing issues head-on, initiating the process of reclaiming both my own sense of agency and that of Yanolja. It's true that everyone experiences moments of doubt, but incorrect decisions during such times don't just affect the individual—they impact everyone around them.

I witnessed what was happening and realized how important I was. Everyone should be the master of their own life and possess a sense of agency. Perhaps I can now say that Yanolja, after ten years, is finally ready to start anew, because, countless times, I have been shaken and gained wisdom from those experiences. On days when my heart and life are shaken, I remind myself that these trials are not the outcome but part of the process; a journey toward success. I remind myself to consider these shakes as divine tests meant to strengthen me. I shall stand tall as the most important being to myself. I shall not give up on living a life with self-agency and self-esteem.

DON'T TRY FOR JUST A FEW DAYS AND GIVE UP OR SAY IT'S NOT POSSIBLE

We have always been changing, just without always realizing it. As adults, there are times when we become resistant or numb to change. This resistance is in stark contrast to our early years. As a baby, we exert effort for a full two years of our life to be able to do simple acts such as flipping over, crawling, standing on two feet, walking and running. We start with mumbling sounds, then gradually learn to say "momma" and "dada," and it takes anywhere from five to 20 years to develop normal language skills. In this way, we continuously strive for change and growth in every aspect of our lives. Whether prompted by others or not, making effort is essential to our life's journey and eventually we achieve what we focus on.

As adults, when you grumble that things don't happen overnight or you give up too easily, or when you find yourself in despair, thinking you are incapable, look back at the path you have trodden. You will eventually make it, just like you did when you learned to walk and talk. People often give up too easily and draw conclusions too soon. In the new year, I hope not to see myself giving up after just a few days of trying. I hope for a year where I can keep up with everyone else's pace, exerting effort and patience, even if it means progressing slowly and steadily.

I am walking on two legs and speaking with my mouth. I know how to use chopsticks, and I can recite multiplication tables. These may seem trivial, but think about the amount of time and effort it took to achieve these feats. Think about how much patience and effort are required for such simple tasks. Given this, it's clear that to achieve something extraordinary, one must be even more patient and put in greater effort. This new year, I resolve to make more effort in everything I do.

January 2, 2014, 08:41

WE HAVE FINALLY BECOME A ZERO
AND STARTED ANEW

Looking back at the last ten years, the most challenging aspect was the organizational restructuring and related personnel changes. In the beginning, I needed talent who could turn my plans into an online business. However, finding the right designers and developers was extremely challenging. In a small company, I could handle everything from finances to marketing myself. But I hit a roadblock in hiring the right personnel, as I lacked knowledge in programming languages and design. Posting job ads on recruitment sites and forums didn't yield positive results.

We managed to recruit a few employees, but they often left our small, seemingly directionless company after just a few days, unilaterally terminating their contracts. Here, the company was on the receiving end of the 'termination' notice. There were also cases where people lacking the necessary development skills joined and made it clear that development was unfeasible. Before completing their probation, the company decided to part ways with them.

This experience taught me that working with technically skilled individuals would be challenging. Eventually, we decided to outsource the development, but even that was not straightforward. Being inexperienced in planning, I had to rely solely on portfolios to assess if someone had the skills needed, often having to judge based on their demeanour. Looking back to when the current vice president of Yanolja, a cofounder, and I started with just two desks, it's incredible how we've grown into a reputable dotcom and mobile company.

It started as a company that provided information online, and we didn't know anything except what we did for the online community, Daum Cafe. We knew nothing about sales, taxes, business management or anything else. All we had was guts. We learned about sales by personally visiting potential customers, gained a little knowledge of taxes by visiting tax offices, encountered the basics of marketing by starting keyword advertising, and learned about HR by conducting job interviews to hire employees. For me, the past ten years have been a continuous journey of learning through personal experience in the field. However, the fact that I, as the CEO, do not know everything has sometimes created difficult situations for our organization.

Every November, we prepare for personnel changes. We spend nearly a month considering what we are lacking and what we need to carry into the next year, observing people and shuffling through personnel evaluations. We conduct interviews and attempt to contact outsiders. By the end of November, we get a rough picture, but it always seems to be a difficult task. If the company has stopped growing or is not starting new businesses, there's no need for more people; just maintaining the status quo is enough.

However, our business, although primarily in the travel and lodging industry, covers online, mobile, and offline sectors and is continuously expanding. It was not easy to decide how to allocate personnel appropriately. We are now organized into various departments like marketing, PR, content, sales, management support, management research, strategic planning, development, quality QA, design, service planning, franchises (about seven departments), new TFT and branch offices (about four departments). But it was initially challenging because this structure wasn't there at the time. There were jobs to be done, but no one knew how to do them. This led to a need for hiring talent, but the process wasn't easy, due to the time, funds, and evaluating the disposition and abilities of people. If I had been instructed to create an organization of 200 people, I couldn't have done it. It grew from two people to our current 200 employees. If we had 200 employees from the beginning, what would I have asked them to do? Having a pool of talent is great, but ultimately, you need a revenue structure to support it.

Ultimately, the reality is that a company can either grow or regress. Operating in the online and mobile world, where service and physical changes happen rapidly, we have to respond constantly to changes. The company needs to keep pace with changes and possess the value to create them. This makes organizational composition difficult. Numerous companies create organizations with various policies and strive for growth or happiness because organizational composition is the foundation for survival and growth.

There are companies that want to work with a sense of self-agency. On the other hand, there are companies where only labour exists, without self-agency. There are companies that will die if they don't stand out, while others will die if they do. Each company's culture and organizational form may be opposite, depending on its characteristics, but the intention of the people who consider this organizational structure is the same: to create a continuously growing company to increase its future value.

Yanolja started like a family. We believed in the importance of strong bonds for survival. While we did value everyone's abilities, we placed greater emphasis on trust and strong emotional bonds. However, the market changed rapidly, evolving beyond what we had imagined. We realized that strong emotional bonds were not enough to keep up with the flow of the world.

Eventually, in 2014, Yanolja attempted many changes and made significant sacrifices for organizational improvement. We welcomed a professional executive and tried to implement change. However, this change from the outside failed because even though the company had been in business for only nine years, we had relied too much on emotional bonds, pushing the company almost to breaking point. I believe it was not the fault of the professional executive, but rather that the way I had been running things for over nine years was flawed. Ultimately, I decided to take charge of improving the internal organization myself and re-entered the company.

I released everyone in the company from their positions, ranks, and the tasks they were doing. It was a painful process, but necessary because the organization was so tangled and knotted with no signs of unravelling. We found ourselves in a challenging situation, unsure of where to go or what to do. Consequently, in the second half of 2014, the company's structure was completely revamped and reset to zero, leading to the rebuilding of today's Yanolja.

During this process, many employees were let go, and some resigned voluntarily to seek better opportunities. Over the span of a week starting June 16, 2014, over 30% of the employees left Yanolja under a voluntary retirement program. The company was left in a comatose state, barely functioning and incapable of responding to any emergencies. With most key personnel gone, we were constrained to performing only the simplest of tasks, unable to pursue more ambitious goals. I had to come to terms with this reality. It's an experience that many would prefer to avoid discussing, but I believe in confronting it. Ensuring that such events never recur is both my duty and responsibility.

This situation could have been avoided if I had demonstrated better leadership, and been smarter and more thoughtful. The entire situation was my fault. Even afterwards, employees continued to leave because they didn't see a future with Yanolja. They must have felt insecure as co-workers were leaving, the internal system was unstable, and there were limitations to what they could do. It was like a time bomb that finally went off. Yanolja found itself devoid of confidence, future vision and the drive to act. But ultimately, we reset to zero and restarted. We identified a direction that would put us ahead of the times. We deeply felt and embraced the direction we truly wanted to take and began anew. The organization is still a work in progress. We will continue to shape it and experiment. Many talents have been recruited from outside. Fortunately, we have accurately identified our new direction.

Managing an organization is always a challenge. Yet, without an organization, we do not exist. Therefore, human resources, the people who constitute the organization, are the most critical part of the company and crucial in determining its future value.

MY BUSINESS CARD IS IMPRINTED
WITH THE TITLE OF 28-YEAR-OLD
'CEO SUJIN LEE'

When I started the business, my business card read 'CEO Sujin Lee.' At that time, I was only 28 years old – a remarkably young CEO. Being young meant that I might not understand the ways of the world, lacked experience, and was not fully capable of being considerate. My perspective on the world was narrow, and I lacked a clear sense of direction. I hadn't yet tasted success and was like a candle in the wind.

Moreover, my starting capital was far from sufficient. Everything was lacking, both internally and externally. But the role of a CEO is clear. A CEO has the mission and responsibility to succeed. In any circumstance, a CEO is given the task of achieving success. Producing results is an essential requirement that must be met.

Thinking, "Let's give it a try for fun" or "There's always another opportunity" is a sure path to failure. And when you fail, it affects not just the CEO, but also those around them. I chose the position of CEO on my own, but the repercussions of failure extend beyond just the CEO. Therefore, a CEO must succeed. Year after year, as I continued in my role, I felt myself gradually developing the necessary disposition. However, the problems I faced as a CEO were always different, challenges I had never encountered before. Each time I faced a problem, I experienced a mixture of nerves and excitement. Sometimes I was hurt by these challenges, and at times, I even regretted my past decisions. But, once again, I started anew in search of future value.

The world changes rapidly, as do business conditions, and people's thoughts evolve even faster. Our market value is reaching unforeseen heights, and its future trajectory is unpredictable. Consequently, no matter how intelligent a CEO may be, it's not always easy to make the right decisions. While Yanolja leads the lodging market as a distinctive company, those within this market keenly observe Yanolja's changes. The CEO of Yanolja must also keep a close eye on changes in other markets, continually adapting to variables and challenges. Such situations arise every single day without fail.

However, there is something that weighs even more heavily on a CEO's mind: talent. In a company, securing talent is the only way to strengthen market dominance. Through talented human resources, a company can acquire clearer data to make judgments about market changes. Recruiting talented human resources, however, is a challenge for small and medium-sized companies. The relationship between the CEO and employees is important, but the relationships among employees are even more so. The ideal condition for a company is when all members of the team move organically, are considerate of each other, and share ideas. Yet, few companies can rest assured when it comes to collabouration.

The human heart is complex, with each person experiencing a thousand different thoughts and actions. A healthy company is one where these diverse elements come together, where people empathize and share, and lead a harmonious life. Over the ten years of running the company, issues such as interpersonal problems, talent acquisition, employee growth and the resulting challenges to the CEO's skills have always been more pressing than market situations. Personnel issues are sensitive matters that could erupt at any moment, even in a company that offers better benefits, higher compensation and a more relaxed work environment.

Even when everything is going well, people-related issues can unexpectedly arise, and this is really disheartening for a CEO. It leaves you feeling hollow and heartbroken. In severe cases, it can even lead to mental distress. But what can be done? Ultimately, the situation must be managed. It's essential to consider the causes and responsibilities involved. Since business is an ongoing process with a long road ahead, you cannot dwell on problems indefinitely. However, hastily or poorly resolving them can lead to further issues and create problems in the team. This, in turn, slows down the company's growth. Moreover, a company is a space for individual survival and a part of everyone's life, so taking sides can easily turn it into a political arena, which is a troublesome situation.

Ten years as a CEO may seem like a short or a long time, depending on one's perspective. During this period, I've had to be the first to sense and adapt to various changes, big and small, such as shifts in the market economy, global changes, changes in lifestyle, and changes in people's attitudes.

Furthermore, I believe that maintaining a stable mindset is of utmost importance. Upon close examination, I found that my mind was usually troubled due to misunderstandings between company members and me, or due to poor relationships among them. Therefore, creating a company culture where everyone supports each other is key. In companies that are not large corporations, paying attention to every employee is also part of a CEO's role. Instead of blaming others, the priority is to find the root cause of these issues and identify what is disrupting the direction. All the responsibility, including the failure to succeed, falls on the CEO.

Being a CEO involves tears and endless contemplation. The eyes and ears of those around me are always focused on me, the CEO. This position wasn't assigned to me by someone else; whether I fully understood what it entailed or not, and it's a role I consciously chose. We are often told not to shift responsibilities onto others. However, I sometimes wonder if CEOs, perhaps more than anyone else, tend to pass greater responsibilities onto others. This leads me to think about whether I should embrace the profession of CEO with more sincerity and an authentic attitude. Being a CEO is the life I desire.

LET'S KEEP IN MIND: TODAY'S DECISIONS CHANGE TOMORROW

Whether in business or not, there are times when we must make decisions. In personal matters, these decisions often involve weighing our own interests, family interests or relationships with friends, leading us to choose the most beneficial outcomes for ourselves. Confined decisions only lead to confined outcomes. In childhood, regardless of whether choices are good or bad, their magnitude is largely influenced by our parents. As adults, we become acutely aware of the consequences our decisions might bring.

As a child, there were many things I wanted to do but couldn't, and many places I wanted to go but couldn't. There were even more things I didn't want to do but had to. However, the responsibility for these actions was not significant. I could start over, someone else might step in or at most, I faced punishment for wrongdoing. But what about when we become adults? Is there someone to take over for us? Does anyone else live our lives? Decisions and their consequences become our own. This realization makes me wonder if we become accustomed to a life where we avoid making decisions or become fearful of their future consequences. Big decisions bring significant consequences, which can lead us to make smaller-scale decisions, delay making them, or conform to societal norms, often blaming society when things go awry.

In my youth, I couldn't rely on anyone. I had to stand up and walk forward alone. This perhaps made me realize the severity of decision-making earlier than others. Decisions can be made quickly and in favour of immediate benefits. However, I soon learned that what seems easy and advantageous in the short term might not always remain so in the long term. Being overly excited by immediate gains or indulging in fantasies and pleasures can be misleading.

People make decisions that perpetuate their poverty, and complain about low salaries. They often fail to make decisions that could alter their situation, choosing instead to continue living in their current reality. They know that their thoughts can bring change, but they do not strive to broaden their thinking. I realized that these situations are the consequences of one's own decisions. Perhaps this ability is the only legacy passed down to me from my parents; after their loss, I was forced to depend on myself.

After founding the company, things changed. Previously, my decisions affected only me, but as the company grew and the number of employees increased, each decision I made carried a heavier weight. Decisions that were once solely my burden, often accompanied by fear and nervousness, now had implications for others as well. Some might suggest abandoning this role to avoid the pressure, but it's not that simple. The business started for monetary reasons, but as it progressed, my responsibilities and sense of duty intensified.

While running the business, I got married and had children. It wasn't my first experience of family, but it felt as significant as if it were. I had to be mindful of the future, not only for my own family but also for the families of my employees. Yanolja has grown, encompassing many lives beyond my own. Additionally, there are our partner companies to consider. What began as a personal endeavour has expanded far beyond that; now, I must make bigger decisions from a corporate perspective, not just as an individual. This is a constant source of concern.

Am I thinking in the right direction? Is this the right approach? What will our future be like? I need to think beyond immediate profits, envisioning and making decisions for an expanded picture of tomorrow, next year, and three years down the line. Plans for ten or 100 years from now aren't really relevant to us because the market is constantly changing. I would like to see our company lead the market, but that leadership role isn't ours yet. My decisions impact the future of the 200 Yanolja employees, their families, and our partner companies. Therefore, although making decisions might not seem difficult now, when thinking about the future, they become endlessly complex and even frightening if there's a lack of certainty.

Over more than ten years in business, I have made numerous decisions, leading to both successes and failures. There were times when the wrong decision, bolstered by the strength of the organization, became a success. Conversely, there were times when seemingly good decisions failed due to a lack of organizational support. While decision-making is ultimately my responsibility, it always involves gaining empathy and a sense of unity. Having power, the highest stake, or the final say doesn't mean making decisions that completely disregard the members of the organization; such decisions, no matter how good, are far from success.

That's why, in moments of decision-making, I am always nervous, but I strive to share the situation and gain empathy. Before turning 20, my actions and thoughts were confined within a certain system or box.

As an adult, I could think within larger contexts and even beyond those boxes – the protective fence was no longer there. The path I wanted to take became the direction I could pursue.

I started my business at the age of 28. Until then, I was a young man who had the freedom to make any decision. My circumstances didn't allow me complete freedom, but the path I wanted to follow remained unchanged. After starting the business and becoming a young CEO, I stumbled through, not knowing right from wrong. Yet, I kept growing the business bit by bit with grit and perseverance. Gradually, what started as a small personal business grew into a small, then medium-sized enterprise. Along with this growth came a better life, but also the expectation to make more complicated decisions and shoulder heavier consequences.

We often thoughtlessly say, "If I were you, I wouldn't have done it that way." But if one were actually in that position or faced with that situation, we would realize how shallow that statement is. Others may focus only on the correctness of decisions, showing interest only in what is right and successful. But when you're in the thick of it, making decisions about an uncertain future rather than based on past outcomes, it becomes apparent that no one can definitively say what is right or wrong.

Of course, there is a sense of right and wrong in decision-making within the realm of common sense, and it's vital to not deviate from that. However, making decisions that transcend current realities and consider the future is not easy, especially when immediate benefits seem more enticing, and the results of those decisions only become clear with time.

But let's be clear about something: the decisions you make now can change your tomorrow. So, take a cool-headed look at yourself, have a clear understanding of your situation, and think about what to do and how to do it. Make decisions that correspond to reality, rather than ones that are far from it. Rather than expecting to change everything all at once, expect changes to happen someday. No matter what happened in the past, I am currently in the process of creating my future. What kind of future can I expect if I don't correct my direction and take action?

PACE CONTROL IS ESSENTIAL TO COMPLETE THE LONG RACE OF LIFE

I worked throughout my childhood. I had to work through college, and although I worked at a defense company instead of serving in the military, I had to strictly discipline myself, from finding a house to making a living. I worked for a company for three and a half years, and then started working as a motel janitor.

At the motel, I worked 12-hour shifts every other day, and it would be no exaggeration to say that I had no real days off. After quitting the motel job, I founded Yanolja and have been in business ever since. You might suggest that I take some time off now that I have my own profitable business, but how much rest does a business really allow its owner? Nonetheless, I had to take deep breaths and relax from time to time. This is because I naturally realized through experience that without doing so, further creativity would be impossible.

Sometimes, I am tempted to unburden myself, kick back and do absolutely nothing. Everyone has days when things don't go well. Occasionally, no matter what you do, nothing seems to work out. What should I do when faced with a mountain of tasks, but my thoughts are disorganized, and I can hardly even move my body? What if it feels like my body and mind are overloaded? I must be bold and unburden myself. To me, relaxing has always felt like a luxury, because doing nothing seems equivalent to leading a meaningless life. However, running non-stop has taught me that not letting go means missing out on doing more. It seems I have developed a self-protective ability to sub-consciously rest when I feel overwhelmed.

Perhaps this is why there's so much talk about a culture where one can earn money while playing. Having experienced that productivity doesn't always stem from working fervently, I believe that work efficiency is enhanced in a more relaxed working atmosphere. Sometimes, when carrying too many heavy loads, I feel overwhelmed. This heaviness hinders my progress and tires me out. Therefore, when I feel burdened or a bit idle, I try to take a step back and rest. After all, life is long. How long can I keep running? Probably until the day I die. Despite saying things like "I'll retire" or "I want to live comfortably," my lifestyle and habits are deeply ingrained. It doesn't seem possible to change them overnight. To last in the long term, there are times when I need to recharge. I must let go to relieve the mental burden. Otherwise, I quickly become overwhelmed again, find myself in situations where I need to hustle, but my efficiency drops and responsibilities become heavier. If I miss the right time to take a break, I risk falling behind and feeling incompetent.

I once challenged myself to run a full marathon course of 26.218 miles. I trained for about three months, completing 6.2 miles after the first month. Then, a month after that, I completed 13 miles, and finally, a month later, the full course of 26.218 miles. I finished the marathon in three hours and 52 minutes. Initially, I thought I couldn't even run, but there I was, completing a full marathon in just three months, and in less than four hours. That was an extraordinary achievement.

It seemed like a ridiculous idea, but I trained every week. As I continued training, my confidence grew. I decided that since I had started, I would see it through to the end. However, on the day of the full marathon, I realized the importance of maintaining my own pace and the necessity of taking moments to quench my thirst at the drink stations along the route.

After running my first full marathon, my body ached for about a month. My legs were swollen, and I couldn't engage in other exercises due to muscle pain and fatigue. It was a completely unexpected after effect. When I first took on the challenge, I was confident that I could easily finish the marathon and return to my daily life without much trouble. Although it was my first race, I had trained consistently and achieved decent records in the amateur competition for the 6.2 miles and 13-mile halves, which made me overconfident.

I ran past the crowded drink station when I should have taken a break, and I started off running very fast from the beginning, trying to beat the record. It was a situation ripe for a face-plant. Arrogantly, I thought I was in peak condition and had received the best training after only three months. Sure enough, from the moment I crossed the halfway mark, I lost all my energy and was overwhelmed by anxiety and nervousness, questioning whether I could even complete the course.

At the 21.7-mile mark, my legs and arms cramped. I was in pain, and I crossed the finish line with muscle patches and gel. With sheer willpower, I managed to push through. My time was much better than I had expected. However, for about a month afterwards, my body endured incredible pain. The sense of accomplishment was short-lived, and I was severely punished for having run too fast. In a situation where I couldn't visit a traditional herbal medicine clinic, get a massage, or engage in any other exercise, my hip joint twisted, and even the slightest activity caused cramps in my legs.

Three months later, there was the Dong-A Marathon. I began training again with Yanolja employees. On the day of the event, remembering the nightmare of my first competition, I ran while taking time for breaks and maintaining a good pace. The result was that my time was one minute slower at three hours and 53 minutes, but I did not experience any leg cramps and had muscle pain for only about a day. There was no issue in leading a normal life and engaging in the sports activities I enjoyed.

Somebody once said that life is a marathon. You run and run, facing gruelling challenges, yet the end never seems to be in sight. That's why pace control is essential. Moments of rest and hydration, catching your breath and quenching your thirst, are necessary to finish the run. While you can train and run marathons multiple times, life, fortunately or unfortunately, offers us only one chance. Therefore, it's even more crucial that while we run breathlessly on the path we've chosen, we also consider efficiency and creativity. When things are tough, or when there's a little bit of leeway, let your brain and body rest for a while.

Looking back at my days as a child, a youth, and as I approached my 40s, it seems my life has been marked by non-stop running. However, at key moments when I needed it, I allowed myself some breathing space. Had I considered that to be a luxury, I can't be sure that I wouldn't have worn myself out. I disagree with the idea that one must run relentlessly just because they are young.

Being young, I think it's wise to occasionally step aside, look around, and think about the future with a broader perspective and mindset. Try to check if you are on the right path and how much energy you have left. If you don't want to worry about that, just spend a few days doing nothing. Something will start to stir in your heart (if there's no stirring, you might have become complacent or too accustomed to a sluggish life, and it's time to get moving). If you feel something subtly stirring during your rest, then you have caught the spark to determine your direction and move forward. I believe this is the path you should walk, and it's the way to your future.

CHAPTER 4

RESTART

2015

ELEVENTH YEAR SINCE FOUNDING: MINDSET

BRACING FOR FAST CHANGES

The year-end passed by quickly. Normally, there would be a message from the CEO at the start of the new year, but there wasn't one this time. Usually, the CEO's work diary is posted around the year-end or the beginning of a new year. But this time, it was missing. Why? Perhaps the CEO was being lazy, disliked writing or had nothing to write about. Maybe all that is true, but the truth is that I wrote something and then erased it.

What message should I deliver? What do we need right now? It would be nice if I could just jot down something that comes to my mind, as I usually do ... But, in the end, whether I wrote a long or short message, I couldn't bring myself to hit the 'send' button. Why? Nothing yet feels familiar – the changes happening at Yanolja, our work environment and even within myself.

Yanolja has been operating in the same way for over nine years. But now, we're trying to change and actually attempt something new, completely disregarding everything we've done so far. Amid these rapid changes, many employees seek answers from me. Can a leader really provide those answers promptly? There was a time when adults complained about high telephone bills from talking for hours on a landline with a friend. Times changed, and people started queuing at public phone booths with pagers, then came the era of making calls anywhere, anytime, with palm-sized flip phones. Now, we live in a time when communicating via social media and mobile messages is more convenient than voice calls.

What will the next era be like? We have been a company that relied on the internet amid all these changes occurring within less than 20 years, and now we have become a company that depends on mobile technology. Yet, the immediate issues are not the leader's primary concern. The greater concern is the inability to predict how the business environment will change three to four years from now, and how the company should adapt to future changes. This is a serious matter. Everyone says it's impressive how Yanolja has grown every year over the past decade, and they wonder how we achieved such growth in the hotel industry.

But isn't this all about the past? Now, standing at a point where even a single year from now causes me concern, I must act to avoid becoming someone who says, "Back in my day!" What have we really discovered? We have discussed many things and tried to find direction in various areas. However, it's disheartening to see us merely convincing ourselves that we won't crumble, without any concrete basis.

"We will definitely succeed!" and "We will definitely grow!"

But what will we do in the end? These days, that is my biggest question. Isn't there a dominant perception that our current reality, while we delay, lacks competitiveness in today's society? The one thing we have is the preemptive brand image that Yanolja has built. But what do we have left if that brand image collapses? Even when objectively comparing services, new companies launching now are perceived as more reliable, lighter and faster than our company. Even if they aren't better than us, how different are they from what we offer? This isn't about blaming anyone; it's a reality we must face.

It's a new year, and we're setting goals for each department, seeking directions to make them happen. However, an issue we need to consider is whether we are still clinging to our past glory of being number one, and whether there is a tendency for selfish competition between teams and individuals rather than collabouration. Shouldn't we seriously ponder whether we are truly embodying the value of being number one, satisfying our customers, and if the path we are on can sustain us three, five or even ten years from now? I'm doing my best right now, but I feel an emptiness inside. It seems the company doesn't fully understand what 'doing our best' means. They say we can do more, but does the company really grasp that reality? From an accurate perspective, if you truly give your all, you shouldn't feel hollow, regardless of the results.

When you try to do your best, it's not about showing off to someone, but about building your own life. The meaning of 'doing your best' should be determined by the customer, not the company. The reality is that a year from now, we could face a situation where, if we don't change, the company could disintegrate. Of course, Yanolja won't go bankrupt. This confidence stems not only from my efforts but also from the hard work of CEO Lim, Director Koo, Director Bae, the executives, employees of each affiliate and every team member who works tirelessly in the field. However, we shouldn't be content with just keeping the company afloat. We should strive to live a life of growth, accomplishment and leisure.

Looking at Yanolja, no one says that the company is offering services that are tangibly refreshing anymore. To survive, we must have the mindset that we can provide such services. The reality is that our company has grown so large that offering tangibly refreshing services has become a challenge, and we cannot deny that we are lagging behind other commercialized services. This could mean that we fear changes, perceiving them not as an enjoyable tool, but as a source of pain.

In 2014, we endured stress and pain amid countless changes. But shouldn't we earnestly assess what we have gained from them? If they only brought pain and patience, then why were all those changes necessary? We must clearly understand what we are here to do, be curious about it, and let that curiosity lead us to find the right way to live. However, even when curious, we don't ask questions, and when problems arise, we often hold our breath instead of seeking answers. We claim to understand the issues, but we tend to compromise with reality rather than strive for mutual understanding.

Consequently, we talk about efficient productivity while engaging in tasks that we don't fully grasp. How can we expect to produce efficiently when we are doing something we don't understand and without a clear reference point for standards? Now, there's only about a month and a half left before we must restart. The days when everything was good are gone. When we seek our comfort, it leads to discomfort for our customers, and their dissatisfaction ultimately puts us in an uncomfortable situation, preventing us from reaching our desired destination. "We are putting a lot of effort into it," they say. So, I wonder how much effort is actually being put in.

Our company is not in a position where common efforts alone can yield desired results. It's a company that might barely survive even with our utmost efforts.

Yet, when they claim to be doing their best, it often seems like a mediocre effort, perhaps because they don't truly understand what 'doing one's best' means. I am not writing this out of blame or distrust. I hope for understanding and not to be misunderstood. For us, it is a time of great desperation. We are an organization that feels we have not enjoyed the changes as much as we have endured them.

However, the world is in a constant state of change, and companies aiming to thrive in this environment are proactively embracing these changes, exerting effort beyond our imagination. We are not alone in this race. Others have started running before us, and startups that joined later are attempting to outpace our weightier approaches with lighter, more innovative services. This is why we must regard the current period as a time of desperation. If we realize this too late, we may have to settle for being a 'chimney company' (a company operating in the lodging industry). We should not fear change but embrace and enjoy it, hoping that this enjoyment will lead to future achievements and a happier version of ourselves.

Others might see me as a rational person, but I am drawn to those who are crazier. I hope for a reality where those who genuinely enjoy themselves and lead change can succeed. Moreover, I hope it's not just an ideal, but that there is neuronal activity capable of leading a super-stimulating and super-positive life in our existence. We all recognize that the biggest problem is claiming we are changing when we are not. What is more powerful than having a comparative advantage is to become incomparable, not because others choose not to compare, but because there is nothing comparable to us.

Our brand is ranked lower than many other competitors, and the notion of comparison makes us feel uncomfortable. Lately, I've realized that even I, as the CEO, am subject to comparisons in the market, with my rank reflecting Yanolja's size and prospects in this hierarchy. It appears that no one can truly escape being compared with others. Therefore, if we don't shine on our own, we might end up being constantly measured against others. I certainly do not want Yanolja to be like that. We are what Yanolja is, and if we underestimate, disrespect and look down on ourselves, refusing to shine, who will acknowledge our brilliance?

As the leader, I can't precisely predict the changes that will come our way. Yet, a leader must set a direction. Now is the time to find that direction, not just by myself but together with all members of Yanolja. I write this lengthy message hoping that everyone will understand. We are striving to change, to create a system that isn't solely dependent on one individual's direction. We have repeatedly concluded that, with our collective thoughts and diverse experiences, we should aim to create masterpieces, not defective products, even if we make only one at a time. It seems we still don't fully grasp why we are undertaking this endeavour.

Rather than making efforts to be recognized by others, focus on efforts that you can praise yourself. Prioritize 'us' over 'me' and recognize that personal comfort can lead to discomfort for others, ultimately making everyone uncomfortable. Transform your mindset so that change becomes not a painful and enduring existence, but a pleasant journey to new horizons. No matter what others say, you can't become someone else. If you don't strengthen yourself, you risk becoming a thorn in the side of our shared space, which would be truly regrettable. Excessive talk about others often reveals a lack of self-confidence.

It is our future, not our past, that is reflected in our current state. That's why the present is so crucial for us. The restart of Yanolja is imminent. We need to embrace change more swiftly, so brace yourself firmly and prepare meticulously. Being recognized may not seem important right now, but understand this: the responsibility for not being recognized lies with you, as does the credit when you are recognized. Be ready to enjoy and lead the changes going forward. This applies to both me and all Yanolja members.

January 12, 2015, 07:54

FANTASIES TURN INTO FAILURES, AND CRISES BECOME OPPORTUNITIES

For me, beginning something has always been a significant challenge. Without starting, there can be no results for anything. Thus, every endeavour our company undertakes must pass through the initiation phase, regardless of whether it leads to failure or success. When I started my business, I did so with excitement and anticipation of success. However, it wouldn't be an exaggeration to say that the journey was fraught with pain.

I realize now that all of these experiences were a vital part of my life, providing precious moments of happiness and creating opportunities for reflection. Yet, the stress related to payroll, sales, development, design, public perception, employees' sentiments, and the overall impact on myself and everything else was unimaginable. Things that I was convinced would succeed often failed. Conversely, situations that felt like crises often turned into new opportunities. This realization led me to apply a certain rule to everything: fantasies often turn into failures, and crises into opportunities.

That's what I repeatedly remind myself when I start a new venture. Am I really caught up in a fantasy, or is this reality? Is this situation an opportunity or a crisis? Of course, even as I write this, I am encountering many new beginnings and business deals. I am using these questions as a baseline for making decisions. However, this does not imply that I can easily discern the nature of each situation or make decisions that are close to being correct. This will always be a challenge for me, as it is for all leaders around the world.

Since starting Yanolja, whenever I faced failure or success, I've had to either quit something or create a turning point to start afresh. The organization always needed to adapt organically, the direction of the business had to shift, and the employees' mindset often required a clear demarcation, aligning with a season or project. The subtle and complex emotions I experienced within these processes often left my brain in turmoil.

Regarding the future, I have earnestly hoped, tried to analyse reality clearly, sometimes left things to chance, and at times indulged in fantasies. I've also had to ward off doubts from those around me who thought I would fail. Looking back, I believe there were two main types of ventures I embarked on: ventures I started with hesitation due to anxiety and ventures I initiated with the expectation of creating a new success story.

Ironically, many ventures that I started with anxiety have achieved successful results. This anxiety compelled me to pay closer attention to my limitations, to identify and address the causes of my anxiety, and to preemptively eliminate risk factors. Conversely, ventures that I began by first writing a success story filled with excitement often did not succeed. Perhaps this was because I was initially more captivated by the dream of success than by a consciousness of the potential risks. This irony becomes particularly poignant now that Yanolja has become such a significant part of my life. However, when embarking on new ventures, I often find myself getting caught up in fantasies. Truth be told, though, who would commit to something while expecting failure? I certainly don't want to focus on ventures I believe will fail. The reason it's crucial to identify as many risk factors as possible in projects that seem likely to succeed is because they are just at the beginning. It's not that they are already successful, but rather that they appear to have the potential for success.

"What is Yanolja's secret to success?"

This is a question people often ask me. In truth, I can't pinpoint exactly how Yanolja succeeded. However, reflecting on my work diary, I noticed that in the initial stages, I experienced more feelings of agony, conflict and crisis than of fantasy. Therefore, I believe Yanolja's growth from a very small company to a slightly larger one was the result of repeated restarts, not just mere beginnings.

Iterative restarting is a critical factor. We all tend to tire easily, so without anything new to invigorate us, where do we find the strength to persevere to the end? We are not scholars; we are just ordinary people. As one of these ordinary individuals, I have consistently chosen to restart with renewed effort when faced with fatigue and frustration due to the lack of long-term resolution.

As a company, we've continuously pushed forward, never being content with our current state, always ready to restart in order to create better quality products with stronger competencies. People usually start with strong resolve and determination. Whatever the task, when you begin, you engrave the commitment to see it through to the end in your heart and mind. However, when challenges arise, a crisis looms, and patience wears thin, the sweet temptation to quit subtly beckons. This temptation may be alluring, but yielding to it could be fatal. This sly temptation constantly lurks around us.

I was so vulnerable, I was often tempted to give up. Fortunately, with many eyes on me, I persisted, albeit foolishly, to reach the end. Thus, we need to segment the path we take. When there's a moment to rest on the journey, or when exhaustion sets in, it's essential to stand up and move forward with the mindset of starting anew. I believe that when all these processes come together, they form what we call life. If you sit down because of a little difficulty, tiredness or a crisis, you'll likely fail. So, consider resting for a while, then stand up and walk again. Approaching challenges with this mindset transforms failure into a temporary trial or pause, not a defeat.

I am ready for a world of new starts, and today's Yanolja has declared another new beginning. The Restart Declaration Ceremony is proof of that. Moving on from the last ten years, much like when we started with only $50,000 in capital, we are making a fresh new start from zero, but under much better conditions – that's what Yanolja's restart signifies. Creating something new is always exciting, but it also comes with its share of pain.

You gain the courage to make a fresh new start when you learn to embrace pain instead of avoiding it. I believe that enduring pain is a necessary process for establishing a more solid future value. Many people try to maintain the status quo because they dislike experiencing pain. They commit to a new start only when pushed to an extreme situation, but even that commitment is often halted by the so-called 'wall of reality.' But reality is not actually a wall. In most cases, you create your own barriers and try to avoid the pain. Even for me, deciding to make a new start and begin from zero again causes a serious headache.

Making a new start involves convincing others and designing your plans according to future changes. You also have to figure out what is advantageous for you, even though you are not a fortune-teller. It requires capital, not to mention time, effort, and collabouration. This means you must let go of your current position. You must stimulate the peripheral nerves of employees. So, a new start is always exciting, but the process is painful. But we know it well: once you persevere through the pain, the accomplishment of success can be yours.

People often ask, "Aren't you making a good living now?" I started this business to make a living. But now that I am doing so, I need to look beyond just making a living and search for something more. That's what 'starting' is about – seeking something that keeps you going, even if it's not solely for survival. In my opinion, this pursuit is the essence of 'starting.' Yanolja has become a company that is always ready to begin anew, a company that embraces pain to shape a favourable future. Let's always remember, "Fantasy can lead to failure, but a crisis can become an opportunity." And we should think, then think again.

"If you don't start now, the outcome will likely be the same or worse." Reflecting on the diary entries I wrote as a boss during the early days of building Yanolja, I feel I can again initiate something with powerful passion.

TOUGH QUESTIONS CLEAR THE MIND

From a very young age, I thought long and hard about how and for what I should live. As a child, I despised poverty and the inability to have many things, fostering a strong desire to escape that situation. Then I grew up. Living each day like a mayfly, life felt overwhelming. Even while working, instead of preparing for the future, I was preoccupied with laughter and chatter, letting days just slip away. Then, suddenly looking back, I realized a year had flown by. With time, I became apprehensive.

"What kind of person will I become in the future?"

Whenever I envisioned my future, it appeared utterly bleak. I found myself in a situation where I had nothing. I feared I would be left with nothing but resentment toward the world – resenting my father, who had left us with nothing, or my mother, with whom I couldn't live since childhood. In fact, resentment had been part of me from a young age.

Eventually, I chose to work in a motel to earn money. As a motelier, I was responsible for cleaning, valet parking, and managing the front desk. Although the job brought in money, it didn't bring peace to my heart. I feared that my youth, pledged as collateral for strenuous physical labour, would dwindle away into my older years.

Thus, I continually asked myself,

"What should I live for?" "How should I live?"

These questions turned into tools for self-reflection and helped me understand who I was. After pondering these questions, I realized a seemingly ordinary truth that was akin to my salvation. My present self is shaped by my past. The actions I take now accumulate, forming the contours of my future circumstances. Once I realized this, I understood how futile it was to simply live day by day, hoping to become someone in the future without actively shaping it.

Let's say I have lived just over 20 years. I maybe have about 60 more years ahead. I cannot afford to spend those 60 years with resentment toward others, harbouring negative views of the world, and being unable to control myself. It's too cruel to mortgage several decades of my life for just a few years of comfort. Yet, many people live like this. They dream of their future selves but continue with the same actions and thoughts in the present, akin to a hamster on a wheel. I began to break away from this cycle. When I found myself becoming lazy, tormented or fearful, I confronted myself:

"Hey, Sujin Lee, how are you going to live? What will you live for? Considering how pathetic your actions and thoughts are, isn't it ludicrous to talk about your future?"

I criticized myself harshly. This led to gradual changes. Initially, self-reproach had little effect on me. For a while, I didn't engage in any self-reflection. But at some point, I began to pity for myself for living such a futile life. Gradually, I started working on changing my attitude and behaviour.

Throughout my business career, I've been plagued with many thoughts. There were times when I couldn't control my intense energy, moments of arrogance where I thought I was the best, and periods of complacency when I would just drink for days. I rationalized these behaviours as part of my job. But you can't deceive yourself forever. I know myself better than anyone else.

Whenever I felt I was wasting my life not being true to myself or felt too rigid and on the verge of breaking, I found myself questioning my actions again.

"What will I live for?" "How will I live?"

These questions hit me like a whip. When I ask myself these questions, they seem to cleanse my cluttered and clouded mind, compelling me to straighten up. It is beneficial to have someone to guide and correct you when you're lost and wandering, but since childhood, I've been on my own, finding my own path. The situation is no different now. As a boss, there's no one to judge whether my actions are right or wrong. Ultimately, I am responsible for creating mechanisms to check, cleanse and correct myself. These questions appear to be the most powerful whip for self-correction.

In my ten years of running a business and 38 years of life, I've encountered countless unsettling situations and endless worries. The question, "What will I live for?" has been pivotal in making me conscious of my existence. It serves as a potent self-rebuke. My past thoughts and actions have played a significant role in shaping my present, and my current circumstances will cumulatively shape my future.

Therefore, isn't it natural to ask myself these questions? I need to continuously reflect on the kind of existence, situation and life I want to lead, especially in challenging times. Initially, it may feel insignificant, and there might be no immediate response. However, by questioning myself, I can discern whether I'm living foolishly, selfishly, lazily, negatively, unhappily, or if I'm truly living well. Talking about the future without this introspection is akin to discussing a lottery jackpot.

How is it different from basing one's future on something as uncertain as a lottery win? My life is mine, and I refuse to leave it to the slim chances and whims of luck, much like a lottery.

Socrates said, "Know thyself." I believe this means that we must understand exactly who we are and strive for growth. "What will I live for?" "How should I live?" These are questions one must obviously ask oneself, and I want to encourage everyone to start right now. I will probably continue to ask myself these questions until the day I die.

ACT! OPPORTUNITIES COME
WHEN YOU EXPRESS YOUR DREAMS

My growth and becoming the master of my life have been fuelled solely by passion. I never lost my passion through my challenging childhood, low-paying jobs, and the demanding life of a motel janitor. I don't boast an impressive education or a prestigious background. All I have is my passion, which has been the driving force allowing me to persevere through a decade in business.

So, what is passion? To me, passion is a continuous and repeated habit. It's the persistence that drives action rather than mere thought, and the determination to never give up until the end. A fleeting effort born from momentary aspiration is not truly 'passion.' Everyone desires to live with lively, vibrant passion, but maintaining such energy is not a simple task. To keep passion alive, one must embrace madness. Those recognized as masters in their fields possess this kind of 'mad passion,' at least in their areas of expertise. Assuming similar starting conditions in a job, how can one exhibit superior skills without this intense dedication? It is only with deeply ingrained passion that one can truly transform the trajectory of their life.

Laziness and arrogance often cause us to forget our passion. I've experienced this myself. There were times when I became complacent, swayed by others' remarks that I had achieved enough success. Sometimes, I indulged in comfort and spent time idly. But I didn't want to waste my life without purpose. Although I am not exceptionally intelligent, I can discern right from wrong. I aspired to create a future better than the present, believing this to be my fundamental obligation in life.

Had I not realized the importance of passion, I might still be living in a fantasy. Passion has the power to turn dreams into reality. A great passion doesn't mean life will transform overnight. However, the passion we hold will inevitably be proven through future outcomes, as our daily lives cumulatively shape that future. Knowing this, how could anyone justify wasting precious time in idleness?

I've observed a common characteristic among successful individuals I've met: they transform their dreams and ambitions into reality. Deep contemplation reveals that everyone can find a way to realize their dreams. However, most people fail to act on these insights. Dreams shouldn't remain internal; they must be brought to life through persistent action. Unfortunately, many realize this truth too late. This is why I feel compelled to express this message loudly.

"Act!"

Remember, you are the sole master of your life. No one else can act on your behalf. Blaming your circumstances or being pessimistic about your current situation won't change anything. Our youth is too precious to be spent idly, letting life slip away.

OPPORTUNITY IS ABOUT BEING READY TO SEIZE IT

It's often said that life presents us with three significant opportunities. Many people regret and lament having let these opportunities slip through their fingers. In my business experience, I've realized that these so-called great opportunities come and go multiple times. The adage of 'three opportunities' is misleading; in reality, they arise countless times and can vanish just as quickly. No matter how appealing an opportunity might be, it is worthless if it's not seized and utilized. Over time, and depending on the circumstances, an opportunity can even transform into a crisis.

Opportunity, therefore, is a peculiar thing. It can either bring fortune or lead to misfortune. There are moments when you must decide when faced with opportunity. Sometimes, like a stroke of luck, it arrives unexpectedly, bringing immense hope and happiness. However, in such cases, I believe this is the result of continuous and repeated dedication to work, where opportunities are created through the process itself.

People often rely on their intuition to decide whether to eagerly pursue something or let it pass. Some believe that opportunities have never come their way. However, in reality, it's not about whether opportunities come or not, but whether one is prepared to seize them when they do. Discussing opportunities is irrelevant if you fail to recognize the ones that have already crossed your path.

Opportunities are often associated with stock investments, lotteries or endeavours that appear to offer quick, significant success. These, however, are merely forms of gambling. True opportunities arise when one focuses on something and dedicates effort to master a specific area. Simply doing nothing or constantly hoping for a big break is a pitiful delusion.

I've met many people and negotiated numerous contracts, and I've reflected deeply on these encounters. There was rarely time to rest. I saw each of these interactions as an opportunity for Yanolja. It wasn't about a single, monumental breakthrough but rather the accumulation of many small achievements that made Yanolja what it is today. I also view our current circumstances as significant opportunities for Yanolja's future. Each opportunity presented its own set of challenges. Had these challenges not been overcome, they would have transformed from opportunities into crises.

Whatever task I undertook, I preferred inexpensive options and found joy in tackling difficult challenges. I might have intuitively understood that transforming inexpensive things into valuable assets and overcoming tough challenges could enhance my competitiveness. Often, I chose a more arduous path than necessary or stubbornly pursued a path better left untaken. Success is vital, yet one cannot expect success in every endeavour. As a business owner, considering the potential failures of any project is crucial, but there's also a tendency not to avoid projects that might seem likely to fail.

When it's time to move forward, one must proceed. If a challenge isn't going to cause severe harm, it's worth taking the risk as it can contribute to the company's growth and provide strengthening opportunities. With this mindset, I began to embrace challenges that once seemed insurmountable and gradually started to succeed. Overcoming these obstacles boosted my confidence. Through these experiences, we built inner strength until we were recognized as skilled experts in our field. That's what Yanolja represents today.

For the past decade, I have lived in a state of constant reflection and will continue to do so. I am always assessing whether a situation is an opportunity or a crisis, and contemplating if a perceived crisis could be converted into an opportunity. Isn't continual contemplation the duty of a boss? In this role, I must always be ready to embrace challenges, as facing them is testament to my ability to act. We strive to perform our best, regardless of the initial conditions, ensuring that the outcome is ultimately favourable.

A president of a company has the duty to grow the business and generate results. A leader who says, "Considering the bad market conditions, we did well" or "It's okay, we didn't do as bad as the market," is the one who should step down. Ultimately, a leader's duty is to grow and produce results in any circumstances. This requires constant contemplation of what constitutes an opportunity, how to take on challenges, and how to collabourate and position oneself advantageously.

THE TWO GOALS I SET IN MY 20S
SHAPED WHO I AM TODAY

In my efforts to escape poverty, I changed many aspects of my life. One significant change was developing a habit of setting very specific goals. Without goals, my impoverished life would likely have remained the same. The world is full of people smarter and more industrious than me. The challenge is, how can I compete with them to build a better life without clear goals? Hoping for success while repeating aimless daily routines is nearly delusional. To grow, one must first plan the specific direction they wish to pursue.

Throughout my life and in running my company, I have set both major and minor goals. Some have been achieved, others modified or discarded. Yet, there have been goals that have consistently guided my life. At 26, in 2003, I set several goals to achieve by the age of 83. These long-term goals, spanning 57 years, remain relevant even after a decade. The first was to amass assets worth $300 million by 83. For a person in their 20s with nothing, aiming for $300 million might seem extremely ambitious.

I was only 26 at the time, and I knew it sounded unrealistic to aim for $300 million. If someone had claimed they were determined to earn that amount, it would have seemed like a fantasy. However, I set myself a 57-year timeframe to achieve this goal and developed a plan to reach that figure. Initially, my goals for each year were modest, but they expanded over time – two years, three years, and so on. Despite sometimes doubting these numbers, I persisted with my plans and efforts.

Now, 12 years have passed, and at 38, according to my original plan, I should have had assets worth $1 million. What's the reality? Combining my personal assets with the value of my company shares, I've exceeded my target more than a hundredfold. I am significantly ahead of the ambitious goal I set in my youth. How did this happen? I believe that as people grow, so do their goals. Goals are dynamic, not static. A target that once seemed unattainable becomes manageable once surpassed. Those who have achieved their goals know the process and are able to set even higher ones, tackling them with greater ease and broader perspectives. The key lies in setting clear and specific goals. I reverse-engineered my goal's timeline to figure out what needed to be done yearly, monthly, and immediately, and diligently executed these tasks within the set timeframe. I started with what was easiest, progressively experiencing success. These incremental achievements accumulated, fueling the motivation to tackle more complex and challenging issues. By consistently meeting these detailed goals and progressively raising the standard, I realized that my ultimate goal was much closer than initially thought, and within a considerably shorter timeframe than planned.

Some might view my goal of amassing wealth of $300 million by age 83 as materialistic. However, money is not the ultimate goal of my life. It is merely a means. The figure of $300 million represents the scale of what I can achieve. I chose this monetary target because it's a clear way to quantify my aspirations, not because I am solely focused on accumulating wealth.

Emotion holds a significant place in my life. If my life were centreed around money, decisions would be based only on practical gains, neglecting emotional aspects. For me, money is a tool to realize the projects I want to undertake and to enhance my life and those of the people around me. In this context, perhaps the second goal I set at age 26 is truly my life's objective.

My second goal is to be remembered as someone who lived a fulfiling life. This goal differs greatly from the first, lacking a quantitative measure. There is no specific standard or deadline to gauge my progress toward this goal; it's about consistent practice in my daily life. While I haven't been a notable philanthropist, my primary aim has been to avoid causing harm to others. Making sure my presence isn't a source of trouble or pain for those around me has been a basic principle. This goal is more important to me than achieving the $300 million.

Life would feel futile if I were known as 'Sujin Lee, the money-hungry,' or selfish for only seeking personal gain. I aspire to be described as humane, decent and a good friend. My life is enriched by the warmth of human support and kind words. Gaining people's trust and making money are not mutually exclusive. The more I focused on treating others with sincerity and avoiding harm, the more people came forward to support me. Being known for good relationships has also helped my business thrive. Ultimately, striving to lead a good life has been beneficial.

During my childhood, I learned that virtue without competence can be a burden to others. As a result, I aspired to be more than just a good person; I wanted to be competent and capable. I ran a business with financial goals to enhance my quality of life, but I was determined not to become enslaved by money. In my 20s, I set two defining goals that have shaped my life and continue to be the key forces in maintaining my life's balance.

2015

ELEVENTH YEAR SINCE FOUNDING: SCALE-UP[1]

RECEIVING THE FIRST INVESTMENT OF $10 MILLION AT A COMPANY VALUATION OF $200 MILLION

I began as a sole proprietor in 2005 and transitioned to a corporation in 2007. At that time, I had limited understanding of the differences between sole proprietorships and corporations. Despite founding a business, my knowledge as an entrepreneur was minimal, and I learned through facing each new situation.

The company faced intense competition but managed to grow steadily, nearly doubling in size each year. It was a small-to-medium-sized venture with a club-like corporate culture, characterized by enthusiasm and positive energy among all team members.

The truth is, our joy and positive energy didn't solely originate from within us. Interacting with customers was immensely enjoyable. We found great satisfaction in seemingly small things: daily event organization, enjoyment, replanning and receiving positive feedback.

When the company was smaller, every detail felt more significant because our work was driven primarily by customer responses. Even during financial struggles and salary concerns, our customers were our lifeline, especially when considering the future. Over time, we began to accumulate more – increasing sales, profits, and even setting standards for accommodation in Korea. Perhaps we started to see ourselves as trendsetters.

---

1   This section is an addition in the revised edition.

This might explain why we found ourselves becoming complacent, believing in our steady growth amid competition. It was an era marked by the emergence of startups, each armed with innovation as their greatest weapon. Initially, we underestimated these small enterprises and their challenges.

We considered ourselves a small yet stable and competent company. However, we were not the best. We had overlooked the importance of innovating for customer usability. Even if there was a willingness to innovate, were we denying ourselves by clinging too tightly to our established ways? This was a question I asked myself. Based on our past business experiences, I had a growing realization that if we continued on this path, our company might either cease to grow or lag in the competitive race, even if it managed to expand.

In 2014, I felt compelled to completely transform the company. Stability was no longer my primary focus. I was convinced we needed innovative challenges and thus directed numerous team members to devise a breakthrough. Although I understand now, back then I did not know the exact path. This led to 30% of our team members departing through a voluntary resignation program, while another 20% left, struggling to adapt to the changing corporate culture, missing the old ways or because their colleagues were leaving.

The loss of half our employees within six months was a turning point in Yanolja's reinvention. It marked the beginning of our journey in recruiting new talent, altering our work methodologies and gradually being recognized as part of the startup community. Naturally, this transition was extremely challenging for many of us.

Moving away from established methods to explore new avenues was mentally taxing.

This period involved relentlessly cultivating a new environment, which meant enduring stress, adapting, learning and growing. It felt like being trapped in a swamp, questioning how long this would last. We were still searching for our path, lacking even a hint of what had fuelled our initial growth and the reasons behind our need to grow.

We had the inherent capacity for growth and were growing despite the circumstances, but it was not a controlled or deliberate process. I strongly believed that without embracing these changes, we would not know our future direction. Consequently, I resolved that securing investment and evolving into a startup was essential for our survival.

In the fall of 2014, I approached Bo-chan (then the CFO and now the executive of finance and management support at Yanolja) and Bon-gil (formerly the Director of Business Operations and currently the founder of the JustSleep startup). I proposed that we should seek our first investment. I tasked them with preparing a single A4 sheet to outline the market size and our current situation, after which we'd meet with investors, assess their reactions, and try to secure investment.

By 2015, many investment firms showed interest in us. However, there were numerous areas where our company wasn't fully prepared for investment. Moreover, there was a considerable discrepancy between the market's valuation of our company and what I believed it to be worth. We estimated our value at $200 million, but investors came back with figures like $60 million, $120 million and $150 million. The internal consensus was skeptical about our ability to secure investment at a $200 million valuation. This view was shared by Bo-chan, Bon-gil, and other team members, especially those recently recruited from the investment sector. Feedback from my contacts suggested that proposing such a high valuation risked negative reception during internal discussions at investment firms.

I found myself in a dilemma over the true value of our company. It had been operational for ten years, was profitable, and appeared to be dominating the market, but it was only just starting to tap into the market's potential. Although I recognized clear potential, I also understood that the market's perception could be accurate. Despite this, my resolve to deeply consider and make more vigorous attempts was firm. The interest from various investors, independent of our company's valuation, signalled potential. It suggested that our presence in the market was seen as an opportunity. Even though we hadn't fully mastered the essence of innovation, we saw ourselves as the organization most likely to revolutionize the Korean accommodation market.

In July 2015, we secured a significant milestone: Partners Invest[2] acknowledged our post-valuation of $200 million and invested $10 million in our company. This was 18 months after we set out to transform the company into a startup. Looking back, it doesn't seem

---

2   Partners Invest initially invested $10 million in July 2015 and followed up with an additional investment of $10 million in February 2016, valuing the company at over $300 million. Subsequently, they sold all their shares to Aju IB Investment, doubling their initial investment.

like a long journey, but at the time, it felt like an arduous, lengthy process. The support from Lee Beom-seok (currently the founder and president of Murex Partners) and Kang Dong-min (then the chief judge, now cofounder and vice president of Murex Partners) was crucial. Although we were congratulated on the investment, the prevailing sentiment in the market was that our valuation was too high and that Partners Invest had taken a considerable risk.

Our debut as a startup, marked by receiving our first investment of $10 million at a valuation of $200 million, was a significant event. While a $10 million investment might now seem standard, back in 2015, achieving such a valuation and investment level was challenging. Many leading startups received investments during that time, but we were not yet in a position to play a leading role in the investment market.

HOW MANAGING DIRECTOR LEE BEOM-SEOK BECAME OUR FIRST INVESTOR

Understanding what it means to be invested in, and to invest, all boils down to trust, which is earned through attitude and respect. There was a lack of trust between many investment companies and us. They recognized our growth, but it fell short of their expectations. I couldn't provide them with substantial indicators or logic to challenge their assessment or convince them otherwise.

It was undoubtedly a time when competitiveness was essential. I was grappling with several conflicts. While confident in our ability to succeed without investment, I also acknowledged the possibility of failure if we didn't secure any. What would our situation be now if we hadn't received that investment back then? At the very least, we wouldn't have achieved our current growth.

One day, I received a call from Managing Director Lee Beom-seok. He suggested we have dinner and engage in a frank conversation. During the dinner, he shared his life experiences, his business aspirations, and his reasons for joining an investment company. He talked about the kind of growth companies should aim for and how he wanted to contribute to that growth. At the time, I must admit, I didn't fully grasp everything he said. But now, I am beginning to understand it, bit by bit. We are growing. Ever since we restarted, I've started to comprehend his perspective a bit more.

Lee Beom-seok confided that he was moved by my hands – the hands of someone who had led an office-based, dotcom, mobile service company for ten years. He noticed how rough and calloused they were, likening them to a farmer's hands. My hands are still the same: dark, rough, with thick, bulky finger joints. They bear witness to my childhood spent helping with farming and housework, to my days as a motel janitor, changing bed sheets and doing other manual labour.

Upon seeing my hands, he said, "These hands are your resume. I believe in them and want to give them a try." He would sometimes talk about his own hands. I appreciated his effort to understand me, his respect for my work, his belief in the market's growth potential with digitalization, and how he valued my hands, seeing them as indicative of someone with the potential to succeed in this field. Thus, I decided that if I were to receive investment, it would be from someone like Lee Beom-seok, not from an investment bank.

I asked him for three promises, which he vowed to do his best to uphold. First, I wanted a valuation of $200 million. Even if the company fell short of this value, I wanted his commitment to do his best. Second, the company needed talented personnel, particularly someone to lead strategy. I asked for his help in recruitment. Third, I wanted his continued monitoring and advice for the company, assuring him I wouldn't view it as interference.

Around March 2015, we were crossing the threshold of mutual recognition. Now, I realize how young and stubborn I was, with limited knowledge. Fortunately, I understood that everything has consequences, and I continuously renewed my resolve, aiming to have no regrets when facing those consequences.

HOW I ESTABLISHED TIES WITH CEO KIM JONG-YOON[3]

Managing Director Lee Beom-seok holds a special place in my heart for his part in our company's journey. After receiving our first investment, I met another key figure who would become a confidante. Right after securing the investment, I asked Lee Beom-seok to introduce me to someone suitable for heading our strategy. This led to introductions to two individuals. One was a leader of a team of 200 members in Facebook's anti-corruption division, with whom we had several video interviews.

The other person I was to meet at our Yanolja office. Despite it being the Korean summer vacation period, he was too busy to meet at any other time. Senior Team Leader Kang Dong-min and Managing Director Lee Beom-seok joined us. Kang Dong-min even took time out from his vacation with his son to be there. This is where I first met Kim Jong-yoon, the current head of business at Yanolja. Kim Jong-yoon is an alumnus of

---

3   Currently, Yanolja is divided into three divisions: Yanolja Platform
    Division (domestic leisure platform business), Yanolja Cloud Division
    (global space management solution business), and Interpark & Triple
    (airline tickets, overseas travel, and entertainment ticket business). CEO
    Kim Jong-yoon currently serves as the CEO of Yanolja Cloud (global
    space management solution business division) and as CSO with strategic
    responsibility for the entire Yanolja Group. Yanolja has a joint consultative
    body called Y-Core, which includes leaders managing each business
    division and the overall direction and strategy of the group. Y-Core plays
    a vital role in supporting the future of the entire company or individual
    business divisions. It offers transparent and honest opinions, discusses and
    makes decisions, and the members collectively shoulder the consequences.
    This structure acts as a unique safeguard for Yanolja, ensuring the
    company doesn't stray off course due to arbitrary actions of individuals.

Seoul National University with an MBA from Dartmouth, and he had worked at 3M, Google, and as a consultant at McKinsey. His connection to Lee Beom-seok was their shared Dartmouth MBA experience.

Before we even began, he mentioned he had read our IR package and investment review committee report. He then proceeded to list reasons why Coupang works and why smaller companies like Yanolja might not. His voice carried a powerful confidence. Although his attitude wasn't snobbish, it wasn't entirely pleasant either. The two-hour meeting ended just like that. He clarified that he attended not out of interest in joining Yanolja, but because he had been asked by Managing Director Lee Beom-seok to meet and offer consultation or explanations.

I had hoped to discuss the lodging industry confidently, but his strong counterarguments left me wondering, "What's with this guy?" Toward the meeting's end, Kim Jong-yoon also stated, "This was a bad investment. I reviewed the investment committee report and couldn't understand their valuation." This brought many thoughts to my mind. Hearing such blunt criticism from someone who had worked at McKinsey and was consulted by large corporations was nerve-wracking.

After the meeting, Senior Team Leader Kang Dong-min was visibly upset and said to me, "Everyone is entitled to their opinion, but his was overly one-sided. Don't take it too personally, and I apologize to you." Managing Director Lee Beom-seok also expressed regret and told me, "I'm sorry, Mr. Lee. This isn't what I expected when I arranged this meeting. It seems I made a big mistake."

After they left, I remained in the office, lost in thought. What went wrong? Am I really approaching business incorrectly? Before the meeting, I felt like our company was at the centre of the startup world, with a host of media interview requests due to our $200 million investment. Considering this, why was his critique so sharp and stinging? Did he genuinely believe that we lacked the capability to address our weaknesses, grow in the market and overcome challenges, no matter how hard we tried?

Why didn't I effectively counterargue or discuss our market situation? When he asked, "Who is your biggest competitor in receiving investment?", I replied, "Perception. When the perception changes, we will spread our wings and transform the company." Yet, where did the confidence in my answer go?

I called Lee Beom-seok and expressed my interest in working with Kim Jong-yoon, asking for his contact information. However, Lee Beom-seok, thinking Kim's blunt words had affected me and assuming Kim wasn't interested in Yanolja due to his harsh critique, suggested introducing me to other candidates. Despite this, I obtained Kim's number and reached out to him for a meeting.

I met him near the McKinsey office in Jung-gu for lunch. Afterwards, he took me to a large corporation where he was consulting, and we had tea there. Our conversation was solely about the industry. If he spoke of reasons it would fail, I spoke of reasons it would succeed. Realizing we needed more time, we agreed to meet again over the weekend. We reconvened in the café on the first floor of our offices.

We talked nonstop about business until after midnight, without even breaking for dinner. The discussion was so engaging that time just flew by. We strategized new business models for the industry. At 1 am, as I drove him home, I said, "Please think over this business model, and if you are sure about it, join our company." I emphasized that what mattered most was not the present, but what we were doing for the future.

Kim Jong-yoon took a hiatus from his CEO role at his company to join Yanolja for three months, working without pay. This period was dedicated to evaluating the strategy we had discussed. He thought about whether our organization could evolve, scrutinized our market size estimations for accuracy and considered whether our proposed business model was viable. Ultimately, he decided to become a part of our team. I attempted to offer some compensation, proposing a temporary salary of $5,000 per month, but he declined, insisting it might cloud his decision-making process about staying or leaving.

"What conditions would you need to join our company?" I inquired.

Kim Jong-yoon responded, "To effect real change, I need to be at the centre of command, not on the fringes. I don't aspire to be a subsidiary CEO; I aim to lead central strategy. Also, while Yanolja may appear to you as a highly capable company, it is still a small startup. I want my contribution to be appropriately valued when Yanolja reaches unicorn status."

Initially, I envisioned him as the CEO of a subsidiary managing reservations, but instead, I designated him as the Vice President of Yanolja's main office.

When Yanolja attained unicorn status, I promised him options equivalent to about 1% of the company's shares. Considering our startup status, I couldn't offer him a salary equivalent to his previous role, so we agreed on a figure sufficient for his living expenses. This arrangement required our utmost effort and top-notch results, as anything less would render our endeavours meaningless. Thus, we formed a formidable team: Kim Jong-yoon, the trailblazing leader; Bae Bo-chan, the best pathfinder I know; and myself, a fighter who never steps back in the face of challenges.

WHAT KIND OF MAN IS CEO
BAE BO-CHAN?[4]

Bae Bo-chan is a master at finding paths. In my view, his most significant attribute is his ability to consistently discover a way forward. Although it may not always be flawless, he succeeds about 90% of the time. I have never encountered anyone quite like him. Initially, I thought he was highly educated, amiable yet competitive, and possibly seen as a prodigy in his youth. However, working closely with him, I've recognized that he has been instrumental in the company's growth.

CEO Kim Jong-yoon excels at trailblazing and has a strong aversion to losing. On par with him is CEO Bae Bo-chan. He is meticulous and can find a breakthrough in even the toughest situations, provided there's the slightest opportunity. Both leaders share a common trait: an inability to tolerate defeat.

I recall drafting the market situation on an A4 sheet of paper.[5] It indicated that there were 33,000 hotels,

---

4 Currently, Yanolja operates as a conglomerate with three divisions: Yanolja Platform Division (domestic leisure platform business), Yanolja Cloud Division (global space operation solution business), and Interpark & Triple (air ticket, overseas travel, and entertainment ticket business). Bae Bo-chan serves as the CEO of the Yanolja Platform Division and as the CFO of the entire Yanolja Group.

5 In our comprehensive survey, we contacted health and hygiene departments of approximately 170 local governments nationwide to gather data on all registered lodgings, including inns, motels, and hotels. The total was just under 33,000 establishments. With each survey, we noted a gradual decrease in numbers, as some businesses ceased operations due to redevelopment projects and regional characteristics. Although it is no longer current, the number has now dropped to below 30,000.

motels and inns, averaging 30 rooms each. * By calculating the daily occupancy rates and unit prices for all 1 million rooms, the annual transaction amount was estimated at $14 billion. Of course, this figure is not exact, as sales are often made in cash or through card payments, with cash transactions not always fully reported in this industry. In 2014, cash transactions were even more prevalent, so this estimate was based on a conservative average of the sales figures I knew about. The average monthly sales per establishment came to about $3,500.

This data pertains exclusively to motels, a sector with a somewhat ambiguous definition. Our business engagements extend beyond motels to tourist hotels, including those with 100 to 200 rooms. Regardless of the exact accuracy, this figure was derived from our survey, and we focused on the expenditure aspect. Our business scope encompassed various expense areas, excluding utility bills, water bills and interest. This included expenses related to private companies but excluded labour costs, laundry, supplies, interior costs, communication, appliances and expenses involving government and public enterprises.

Our target business territory, which could be digitized, was identified as the range of expenses minus the rate of return in the lodging industry. I tasked him with developing a logic to align with this framework, focusing on the areas where we could generate sales and impact.

So, on a single A4 sheet, I outlined the market's transaction size, expenditures and costs for necessary interior renovations over five to ten years. Despite these extensive expenses, our business target comprised a very small segment of the market. Yet, we were perceived as leaders in our industry, highlighting our significant potential for business expansion. This was the key point I emphasized to Bae Bo-chan.

I also suggested that these details should be a part of discussions in meetings with investors. This approach marked the beginning of Yanolja's reinvention as a startup. From then on, while Kim Jong-yoon conceptualized all of Yanolja's business strategies, it was Bae Bo-chan who diligently worked on developing, verifying, and ensuring the feasibility of these strategies.

In a relatively short time, Yanolja achieved a corporate valuation of $10 billion, receiving a $2 billion investment from SoftBank's Vision Fund 2 in 2021. This was a remarkable leap from the initial investment of $10 million at a valuation of $200 million in July 2015. In just six years, we reached decacorn status, with a valuation of $10 billion and a total cumulative investment of approximately $2.4 billion.

For a small startup to attract an investment exceeding $2 billion, the extent of financial, accounting and tax scrutiny it must undergo is immense. Bae Bo-chan was instrumental in managing all these aspects, establishing and maintaining the most realistic standards of responsibility and duty for the corporation.

CEO Bae Bo-chan joined Yanolja in early 2014. In 2013, I recognized that for Yanolja to grow further, we needed field professionals. I believed that surpassing our internal standards and meeting global benchmarks was essential for significant growth. During our recruitment for C-suite positions, one applicant with an impressive and diverse background caught my eye. Many applied, but his resume was particularly notable. He was a KAIST Department of Biological Sciences graduate, had served as an Air Force management officer, and worked at both Samil PWC Global Market Headquarters and Samjeong KPMG IT Industry Headquarters. His varied experiences made me curious about his interest in our company.

He shared that after reviewing Yanolja's financial statements, he saw potential for future growth. His application was driven by curiosity about our unique culture and industry structure. Post-interview, I was convinced we should collabourate. I arranged a meeting with Director Koo Bon-gil, responsible for general planning, to gauge his intentions. However, he wasn't initially interested in a job change. Nonetheless, he communicated his decision respectfully, clarifying it wasn't a reflection of his view of our company. I requested a few more meetings, hoping to build rapport over casual drinks and in-depth discussions. Following these interactions, including a dinner where he became more familiar with the company's situation and culture, and several months of consideration, he eventually decided to join Yanolja.

Bo-chan arrived, almost as an answer to our prayers for talented human resources. Right off the bat, he showcased his prowess by identifying ways to save over $400,000 in taxes. He pinpointed areas eligible for government support and overpayments in tax, thereby saving an amount that significantly exceeded his annual salary. His immediate impact was testament to his value and reliability. This marked our transition into gearing up to make substantial progress. As CFO, Bo-chan has been crucial in shaping Yanolja's financial framework and fostering growth, a fact that is indisputable.

I'm reminded anew of how Yanolja's journey has been shaped by the contributions of each team member, whether in the spotlight or behind the scenes.

EPILOGUE
TO MYSELF AND MY READERS

The onus of living in or transforming your environment rests entirely with you. Even in challenging circumstances where immediate change seems daunting, initiating a new beginning is imperative. We have ample time.

There's another day, another month and another year – perhaps even more time than that. However, we often find ourselves reflecting on the past, either regretting the present or feeling remorseful. It's vital to remember that our investments today shape our tomorrows. Yet, we occasionally lose sight of this, seeking solace in our past. Living excessively future-focused, without appreciating the present, can lead to a constricted life. The key lies in relishing the present while staying conscious of the future; maintaining a harmonious balance.

If the future you're heading toward fills your heart with passion to the point of bursting, why wait? If not today, there's always tomorrow. Just hold on and don't let go, because yielding isn't the attitude to live your life. Overcoming challenges and tackling trials with confidence is testament to our faith in the time we've been given. Avoid pessimism; it alters nothing. The more you indulge in it, the more the world reflects that pessimism back at you.

When you're uncertain about how to change, how to improve your life, and how to brighten your future, focus just 1% more than yesterday. Strive for even a 1% improvement. The greater the challenge, the more positive energy you need, along with a smile just a bit wider than yesterday's. How many of us really know what needs changing to thrive? How can anyone determine how to make a better future without first living in the present? Nevertheless, isn't it better to strive for a life that's better tomorrow than today, rather than just better than others?

You should aim to improve and lead a life that's better tomorrow than it is today, regardless of others. Being too concerned about others' perceptions can lead you to emulate them, eventually living a life that mirrors theirs. Be aware of how you're perceived, but don't let it control you.

You only live once, and your face, body and name belong solely to you. We can't afford to neglect our most precious assets with flimsy excuses about our circumstances. You are a resilient and tenacious force of life. The past doesn't define you; the present moment is the beautiful beginning of your life.

A new day is dawning. Let's begin anew.

August 10, 2015, 07:24
It's Monday morning, and the air is wonderfully refreshing.

Sujin Lee, at the desk in the office of the company that features in my thoughts the most.

ADDENDUM
I WHOLEHEARTEDLY ROOT FOR CEO SUJIN LEE, WHO RADIATES GENUINE HUMANITY

Sujin and I embarked on our business journey together a decade ago, but our first meeting was 18 years ago, in March 1997, at a university tennis club. My senior, Sujin, was lean and tanned, and initially we didn't click. Post-classes, we'd sweat it out playing tennis and often wind up at Goeul Restaurant, a local makgeolli place near the university. Our seniors would treat us to drinks with what little money they had. Sujin was no exception. Often, he borrowed 5,000 to 10,000 won from classmates, always repaying it by the weekend. I later found out that he managed to repay by working hard over the weekends. This showed me his meticulous approach to finances.

As time passed, we grew closer, sharing work, conversations, laughter and fun. After college, Sujin joined a defense company, and I joined the army. When I visited Seoul on leave, seeing Sujin diligently save every

bit of his earnings for his dreams while working in the defense industry made me reflect on myself.

After my military discharge and while job hunting, I heard rumours within our club that Sujin was prospering in Seoul. Curious, I called him and learned he was working in a motel. When I asked if the job was tough or scary, he just laughed it off, saying, "I think you'll do well."

Little did we know, this would mark the beginning of Yanolja. After moving to Seoul, I failed a motel interview, spent a night in a jjimjilbang and eventually landed my first job in Seocho-dong. In Seoul, where I knew no one, I saved money by working in a motel. Sujin occasionally scolded me for frivolous spending. I admired how he maintained his frugality, wearing the same parka for over four years and even depositing as little as 1 cent into his bank account. Our usual meeting spot was a jjimjilbang, where we felt most at ease. It was there that we often talked about our dreams and the future. This jjimjilbang was where Yanolja was conceived, and where our business ideas sprouted. For that reason, the jjimjilbang holds a special place in our hearts and gratitude.

Yanolja's business journey began in a humble apartment in Uijeongbu, which belonged to an outside director. Our office had just two desks. It was a period marked by endless challenges and darkness, yet we embarked on this path with youthful spirit and passion, ready to face any challenges that came our way. Living through those times was tough, exhausting and anything but leisurely. We constantly relied on each other, made promises, and cheered each other on.

The past decade has been fraught with many difficulties. There were times when employees left en masse, leaving only Sujin and me. We also lost the trademark rights to Motel Tour (Motu), which was just breaking even, to a competitor. People we trusted embezzled funds and fled. Each challenge was daunting and draining, but Sujin maintained his integrity and remained committed to his role. His entire focus and energy are still invested in Yanolja, constantly thinking about how to provide quality, user-centred service.

I often tell him to take care of his health, to spend more time with his daughters and to take breaks, but he ends up causing me more worry. I see him more often than my own family. He is my life's mentor and lifelong business partner. Today, as always, I passionately root for CEO Sujin Lee, a down-to-earth man who truly embodies humanity.

IM SANG-GYU
COFOUNDER OF YANOLJA